Every Parent's Guide to Common Childhood Illnesses

PEDIATRICIAN:

Ralph Berberich, M.D.
Ann Parker, M.D.

All rights reserved under International and Pan-American
Copyright Conventions. Published in the United States
by Pantheon Books, a division of Random House, Inc.,
New York, and simultaneously in Canada by Random
House of Canada Limited, Toronto.

Library of Congress Cataloging-in-Publication Data
Berberich, Ralph, 1942—
The available pediatrician.
Includes index.
1. Pediatrics—Popular works.
I. Parker, Ann, 1942—   .
II. Title.
RJ61.B453   1988   618.92   87-43015
ISBN 0-394-56298-4
ISBN 0-394-75509-X (pbk.)

Illustrations and book design by
Marysarah Quinn and Tasha Hall

Manufactured in the United States of America

First Edition

THE AVAILABLE
PEDIATRICIAN

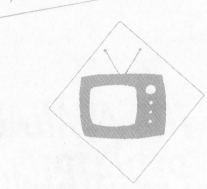

THE AVAILABLE

🏛 Pantheon Books New York

Contents

To
Martha and Jennie Berberich
and
Mike, Jessie, and Andrew Parker

Acknowledgments

The authors owe a debt of gratitude to their families, who put up with them during the preparation and editing of the manuscript. Any occasional lapses of grace or patience on our part were more than compensated for by their fortitude and timely encouragement. Our editor, Sara Bershtel, and copyeditors, Frederica Templeton and Louise Stallard, became both the bond and catalyst for our work. Without their labor, and the unflagging help of Julia Bogardus and David Frederickson, the true malarticulation of ideas and turgidity of prose produced by two physicians trying to write a book would have been revealed for all to see. Our associates, Jane Hunter, M.D., and Steve Kowaleski, M.D., and our office staff, Judy Alley, Bonni Hart, Lanice Clark, Nancy Marchionda, and Amy Marrone, indulged us and helped review the manuscript. We thank our colleagues Barbara Tittle, M.D., Ann Petru, M.D., and Abigail Givens, M.D., who reviewed the manuscript. Harry Strauss first reintroduced one of the authors (FRB) to the inherent simplicity of the English language. The authors wish to recognize two colleagues and mentors who embodied the finest examples of excellence and compassion in patient care: Lewis Meyers, M.D., and John W. Raker, M.D.

A Note to Parents

Although we pediatricians are called "health-care providers," it is really you parents who provide most of your child's health care. You are on call twenty-four hours a day; you know your children best and are usually first to notice when they're not feeling well. When treatment is prescribed, you generally administer it.

Most parents show good judgment when it comes to treating their sick child, but they often worry that they are not doing the right thing or not doing everything that should be done. There are many books that describe sickness in childhood and offer advice on treatment, but we find that most parents do not like to turn to books when their children are actually ill. They feel worried, rushed, inexperienced, and while books may have a lot of technical information, many of them do not answer the important, simple questions that parents ask. Parents often wind up calling their pediatrician as much for reassurance as for information and advice. They want to know what the normal course of illness is, what symptoms they are most likely to encounter, when to take things in stride, and when to worry.

Some of the questions we hear most often are: How

serious is a fever? How high should a child's temperature be before the doctor is called? Can fever or convulsions cause brain damage? Should a baby travel on an airplane if she has a cold? Should a child swim with an ear infection? Can a child catch his friend's ear infection? Can children become immune to antibiotics? When does abdominal pain mean a child may have appendicitis? Can an immunization actually give a child the illness it was supposed to protect against? In this book we have tried to anticipate and answer such questions, offering the kind of basic information that will help you approach your child's illnesses with knowledge and confidence. Ours, therefore, is a book for you to read *before* your child gets sick.

By giving you information about common childhood illnesses and hazards before they occur, we hope to make it possible for you to identify the source of your child's distress and make an informed judgment about its severity. Then you will have a better idea of when to treat a child at home and when to seek medical attention. For example, you will learn that a child who has a temperature of 105 degrees but is active and bright, sleeping and eating, is not as seriously ill as another child with a temperature of 102 degrees who lies still, moaning and unresponsive. If your six-year-old complains every day of a headache before school but has no other symptoms, you will learn to suspect that separation anxiety rather than a neurological problem is probably the cause. Asking the right questions and knowing how to interpret the answers will greatly increase your ability to respond confidently and effectively to the health problems that are bound to arise as your children grow up.

We have also tried to provide some armor to shield you against well-meaning but often misguided advice. Most parents recognize that a cold is not an emergency, yet they must live with their child's misery day after endless day. At the drugstore they are faced with a vast array of over-the-counter cold remedies; television assures them that "Nine out of ten doctors recommend . . ." A neighbor swears by vitamin C and Grandma pushes chicken soup. Meanwhile, the day-care center is running out of tissues. What you need to know in this situation is how to make your child as comfortable as possible and when a visit to the doctor is useful or warranted.

In this book, we have focused on conditions most commonly encountered in children up to age twelve, even though pediatricians often care for teenagers and college-age patients as well. Some diseases, like mononucleosis, which usually affect older children, often occur earlier, so we have included them here. But in general we have not tried to deal with the illnesses of teenagers in any comprehensive way.

We have attempted to give you a solid grounding in simple pediatric care, but remember that no book could or should be a substitute for the relationship a family establishes with its doctor. We urge you to use this book as a guide but to contact your child's doctor for advice and information whenever you feel the need to do so. We hope that by giving you a clear idea of the health problems your child may have and what you can do about them, this book will help relieve the anxiety that all parents feel when faced with the distress of their sick or injured child.

A note about gender: Faced with the undeniable fact that half of all parents and half of all pediatrics patients are female, and that nearly half of the pediatricians in the country are women, we thought it would be best to reflect those proportions in the text, and sometimes use *she* and sometimes *he* for all parties. But the possible combinations and permutations were so many that the result, while undeniably nonsexist, was also confusing; in the end we decided to use *he* throughout for anyone not specifically a mother or a daughter. The decision was reluctant, and we assure our readers that we do not intend to slight the females, or to imply that only males get sick.

Ralph Berberich, M.D.
Ann Parker, M.D.

THE AVAILABLE PEDIATRICIAN

The Healthy Child

*I*t often comes as a surprise to parents that healthy, well-nourished children will probably have a lot of minor illnesses as they grow up. We have come to expect kids to remain well, and it's easy to fear that something terrible must be wrong if they have a series of sicknesses. But colds, ear infections, and diarrhea really are part of a healthy child's life. Moreover, normal events such as teething, constipation, and falling can produce pain or discomfort without indicating any illness at all.

As any pediatrician will tell you, there's nothing unusual about a child who has a number of colds and ear and eye infections a year. Sore throats may recur several times in a few months without being very significant. A persistent cough can afflict a generally healthy child. Gas, loose stools, and spitting up are all normal parts of childhood. Cradle cap and other minor skin irritations come and go. A fever can appear for a day or two and recede without causing any harm.

But how much illness is "normal"? And when does illness suggest lowered resistance or generally poor health? In answering these questions, a pediatrician considers the child's age, the degree of exposure to other potentially sick children, and the nature of the illnesses. Colds, for example, may recur many times throughout childhood and mean nothing at all. That's because colds are caused by many different kinds of viruses, and the body does not have the opportunity to mount an immune response against all of them.

Babies are born with some protection against disease: certain antibodies are passed from mother to fetus across the placenta and remain effective in the baby's body for about three months after birth. A baby's own immune system only develops gradually, forming antibodies as it is exposed to various germs and viruses. Hence, newborns are naturally susceptible to most infections and should not be exposed to crowds or to people known to be ill.

Breast milk provides some protection against infections because it contains the mother's antibodies as well as infection-fighting immune cells. An infant, especially one who is breast-fed and has no siblings, may go for months without a single illness. But give that same child a brother or sister or other children to play with, and before you know it, you're dealing with a series of colds, ear infections, and digestive upsets. When a baby is first exposed to other children—and thus to new viruses and bacteria—he may get sick as often as twice a month. This first period of exposure may last six to nine months or even longer—it often feels like an eternity. But it does pass.

As a child's world expands, a whole new array of sources of infection present themselves. Day-care and play groups offer many benefits to young children and working parents, but they also increase the chances of infection. It is not uncommon for preschool children to get eight to ten colds or other minor illnesses a year. Germs are passed from one child to another by coughing, sneezing, and hand-to-mouth contact. Crowding into confined quarters and sharing toys and bottles increases the incidence of contagious illness. Having feeding and diapering areas too close together may lead to the spread of infections through contamination of food by fecal matter. Furthermore, the bacteria responsible for certain conditions, such as ear infections, tend to be relatively more resistant to antibiotics in day-care populations because one child or another is usually being treated with antibiotics, and only the more resistant bacteria survive to be passed to his playmates.

School-age children commonly have many colds, ear infections, sore throats, skin infections, and a variety of viral diseases with fever. They get chicken pox, headaches, warts, bruises, and broken bones. Some problems are related to extracurricular interests, such as swimmer's ear, neck sprains in gymnasts, scrapes in skateboarders, and poison oak in those who explore the great outdoors. Children between the ages of six and twelve begin to relate to their peers in new ways and become more autonomous. Some no longer feel entirely comfortable having their parents supervise washing and grooming. Some begin to take new risks personally, socially, and in sports. The trick for parents is to set limits for safe behavior without interfering unreasonably in experimental but harmless activities.

Preteens and adolescents have many of the same problems—and some additional ones. Acne can lead to shyness and withdrawal, and self-conscious teenagers may spend months trying a variety of salves and lotions before telling their parents they want to see their doctor. In fact, self-consciousness often leads teenagers to suffer needlessly. Cosmetics and hair sprays may provoke allergic reaction; shoes selected for appearance rather than for fit can aggravate ingrown toenails. Smoker's cough, sexually transmitted diseases, and drug effects signal experimentation that may require an increased degree of parental awareness and intervention. Sometimes it helps teenagers just to know that their parents care enough about them to try to block truly dangerous behavior. Looking at their strapping son or blossoming daughter, parents may feel that routine health checks have become less important than when their children were little. Most pediatricians, however, believe that the combination of vulnerability and increasing independence in teenagers makes regular examinations even more important than they were before.

Even when parents know that a certain amount of illness and injury is to be expected as their children develop, important questions remain: When does a condition become *serious?* When does frequent illness mean that something is really wrong?

In fact, there are only a few situations that make us worry: a series of deep-tissue bacterial infections (such as pneumonia or meningitis), weight loss, decreased appetite, declining activity, increasing fatigue, pallor, or listlessness. In such situations, simple tests can usually determine whether further investigation is warranted. In short, it is not the frequency of illness, but its effects on the child's overall health, that should cause concern.

Though parents worry about how often their child gets sick, their most common concern is whether they'll recognize when their child is *really* ill. "Is my child sick?" is not always a simple question to answer, because recognizing illness in children is not always an easy task. Sometimes parents recite a list of symptoms—he feels hot, looks flushed, has slept longer than usual—and asks us whether their child is about to come down with something. There is often no way to answer to anyone's satisfaction. For some children and for some illnesses, the first signs are obvious, such as fever or vomiting. In other cases symptoms may be subtle, such as vague listlessness or diminished appetite. Some children have their own characteristic early-warning signs of illness, such as a headache or unexpected crankiness. Other children tend to develop specific sicknesses at certain times of the year or in conjunction with certain activities, such as allergies during the pollen season and swimmer's ear at camp. To further complicate matters, the intensity of the symptoms may not indicate the severity of the illness. A seizure due to fever is dramatic and frightening, but usually has no serious aftereffects. On the other hand, a slow loss of orientation and responsiveness after a head injury may mean serious trouble.

Children also signal the presence of illness in different ways at different ages. Infants may wish to nurse more often but lose interest in solid food. They may also become less active and pay less attention to their environment. Babies less than a year old may become increasingly irritable. They cry louder and more often.

Toddlers about to become ill often seem more easily frustrated than usual. They may be anxious and confused when sick. Most of them still cannot explain what ails them, and both parents and toddlers become impatient with their inability to communicate adequately. Once the symptoms are obvious, parents who have responded with impatience feel terrible! But try not to; normal toddler behavior so often includes tantrums, clinging, whining, and sleeplessness, it's easy to miss the signs of impending sickness.

Preschool-age children can sometimes describe their symptoms, but with great variations in accuracy. They often cannot localize the site of the pain or express their degree of discomfort. Doctors are used to seeing children writhing in pain one minute and miraculously restored to their normal energetic selves the next. It is not unusual for a child who has been ill for hours or days suddenly to turn around and say, "I want to play now!" Conversely, another child with a modest fever and minimal complaints will be found to have a raging ear infection that makes the pediatrician wince when he sees the eardrum. Other preschool children are frightened by illness, worried when they do not feel well, and impatient to be "all better."

School-age children usually describe their symptoms quite well. Often they are anxious about the duration and outcome of even a minor illness. They begin to sense and resent the impact of sickness on their daily lives. At this age, some children exhibit physical symptoms when they are worried or have emotional problems; conflicts at home or at school may manifest themselves as headaches, fatigue, or stomach upsets. As children grow older, their responses to sickness often reflect their concerns about body image and self-esteem and the tension between their feelings of fragility and invulnerability. For example, a twelve-year-old with a facial rash may not go to school for several days because of overwhelming embarrassment. Expressions of nonchalance, procrastination, denial, or defiance may belie substantial fear about an imagined serious disease. Older children sometimes misconstrue tidbits of information picked up from friends or from television. They may exaggerate their symptoms or be secretive to the point of endangering their health. They may also show unexpected maturity, sharing both their fears and confidences with their parents.

Just as children react to illness according to their age, maturity, personality, and home environment, parents also vary in their level of anxiety, knowledge, and confidence. Ideally, as parents gain experience, they learn to mix concern and observation with reassurance and nurturing. They are careful not to project their own fears and frustrations on a sick child. Parental calm can often help reduce whatever fear and discomfort a child is experiencing. At times, when both the illness and the child's needs seem unrelenting, the exhausted parents may wish they could simply escape worry and responsibility for a while. Such feelings are natural; it is important not to feel guilty when tired and overwhelmed.

Knowing the most common needs of sick children at various ages will help parents provide appropriate care. Babies need active comforting and respond best to quiet holding, rocking, and nursing. Soothing speech or quiet singing may also be reassuring. Because toddlers tend to assert their independence they may be harder to comfort. The child who says "No!" and "I don't want it!" may still respond very well to cuddling and indulgence. Some toddlers like to scold their sickness in an attempt to control it. Since young children think in concrete terms, identifying the illness with a name and talking about it can be helpful. It may also be useful to talk about when the condition will go away and how much better the child will feel when it is gone. One might ask a child, "What do you want to tell this bad old cold that's making your throat hurt?" The response might be, "You bad cold, go away now or I'll bite you and spit you out!"

As children become more articulate, they need their parents to listen to their expressions of worry or unhappiness. If you are open and accepting, your child will feel able to come to you for comfort and reassurance. When he does come, be sure not to seem rushed or distracted. Older children are very sensitive to atmosphere and will fall silent if they sense that their parents feel uncomfortable or unconcerned about their anxieties. But worries that are not expressed may not go away. A child who seems particularly preoccupied and uncommunicative with his parents may benefit from talking to his pediatrician privately. You may find it wrenching when your child needs and develops a confidential relationship with his doctor, but it is a sign he is growing up, becoming a young adult. Finally, remember even a child who looks nearly grown up needs cuddling and tender loving care —just like the rest of us.

How should parents treat their sick child? Many of us grew up hearing such sayings as "Sick children belong in bed" and "Feed a fever and starve a cold" (or is it the other way around?). Some people believe that one should turn up the heat and wrap up a feverish child. But such practices do not necessarily help and may actually increase the child's discomfort. You can usually trust children to regulate their activities and eating patterns according to how they feel. There are exceptions, to be sure: the child who overcomes overwhelming malaise and fatigue to go to a party with a 102-degree fever, or the child with vomiting whose thirst leads him to drink prematurely, or the dehydrated baby who feels too weak or uncomfortable to drink. Keep in mind that most children lose their appetites when they are sick and should not be pressed to eat as long as they are drinking enough liquid. As illness subsides, these children typically make up for lost time and regain weight rapidly.

When it is necessary to give children medication, many parents are amazed at the amount of cajoling, patience, and persuasiveness required to accomplish this seemingly simple task. Drug companies do their best to make their products as tasty and attractive as possible. (Be sure to keep all medicines securely out of the reach of children because toddlers can confuse medication with treats.) Many times, however, children will not be fooled by pretty colors, and as the spoon approaches those chenched lips and teeth, parents are given that grimace that says "I won't!" As you prepare for battle, check to be sure that you are giving the right medicine in the right dose. Explain that taking the medication is not optional if your child is old enough to understand. Ask the pharmacist if the medication can be given with food or liquid in case you need to disguise the taste. Use a medicine dropper or special medicine syringe for infants. For older children a medicine spoon or cup may work better. Older children can also use a regular teaspoon (which should hold 5 ml of fluid) or take chewable tablets. Most children six years old or over can swallow pills. If a child spits out a medication within ten minutes, it can probably be given again without risk; but if the interval is longer, check with the doctor. When in doubt, it is safer to wait until the next dose is due.

Quiet firmness—not negotiation—may be required to get a child to do what's best for him. A toddler of two or three who refuses medication should be sent to a time-out spot, such as his room, with the understanding that he can come out only when he takes his medicine. In younger children, restraint and force may regrettably be necessary to get the medicine down. Older children may also resist restrictions imposed for health reasons and try to argue and barter about social events, sports, and school attendance during an illness. It is important to be flexible but firm when a real health risk exists.

Considering all these challenges, it may seem like a minor miracle that sick children get better. Take heart. Parents do learn how to recognize and take care of illness in their offspring, much as they learn how to diaper a baby or to sense when their toddler needs a nap. And children do bounce back fast, recover their energy, and regain the wonderful sparkle and verve of childhood.

Being Prepared

*I*t's hard to think clearly when your child is ill and you are worried. A parent's best protection against panic is to be prepared. It's a good idea to have the information and supplies you will need *before* your child gets sick. It's important, too, that babysitters and other caretakers be familiar with your provisions for emergencies.

An important part of being prepared is to have a list of essential telephone numbers and information about your child handy. The list should include the telephone numbers of your child's doctor and dentist, the pharmacy, the nearest hospital that provides emergency service to children, and the nearest poison control center, as well as your local emergency numbers for police, fire, and ambulance (911, or separate numbers). It should also include both parents' work numbers and the names and numbers of friends or relatives to be notified if the parents can't be reached. Your own home phone number should always be clearly indicated so that it can be read off by anyone in a moment of panic. This precaution is especially important since many modern telephones do not have a place to display a number. Important information for the emergency sheet includes the child's age and approximate weight, special conditions or drug allergies that a doctor or nurse unfamiliar with your child would need to know, and the location of medicines and emergency supplies.

Here is a form to make this task easier for you. We suggest you copy the sheet, fill in the information (in pencil, since it will change periodically), and put it up near the telephone where it will be easy to see.

When you call your doctor, state the problem as briefly as possible. *If you are calling with an emergency, please say so at once* to avoid being put on hold by an overworked receptionist or switchboard operator. Be sure to give your child's age and approximate weight (since most medications are prescribed according to weight), and have the telephone number of your pharmacy ready. This important information saves everyone time and trouble.

It is a good idea to keep a few medications on hand. Not many. Most problems resolve themselves without the use of drugs. Time, patience, and comforting heal many minor ills. Moreover, by keeping a home pharmacy small you reduce the hazards of accidental poisoning. We recommend the following:

❑ Syrup of ipecac—for poisoning. It induces vomiting when a child has ingested a toxic substance. Details about administration are given in the chapter on poisoning. Although you should check with your child's doctor before giving ipecac, it saves everyone time and grief if you have it on hand.

EMERGENCY INFORMATION

Child's Name   Age   Weight   Allergic to

_____

_____

_____

_____

OUR TELEPHONE NO. _____

Father at work _____   Telephone No. _____

Mother at work _____   Telephone No. _____

Or notify _____   Telephone No. _____

Doctor _____   Telephone No. _____

Dentist _____   Telephone No. _____

Pharmacy _____   Telephone No. _____

GENERAL EMERGENCY TELEPHONE NO. _____

Fire _____   Telephone No. _____

Police _____   Telephone No. _____

Ambulance _____   Telephone No. _____

Emergency room _____   Telephone No. _____

Poison control center _____   Telephone No. _____

Location of medicine cabinet _____

_____ key _____

❏ Acetaminophen (Tylenol, Panadol, Liquiprin)—for fever and pain. Acetaminophen is safe when given in appropriate doses and intervals, but an overdose can be dangerous. It is important to read the label carefully since the strength will be different for drops, elixir, and tablets, and the dosage will vary from brand to brand.

❏ Antihistamine (Benadryl)—for allergic reactions. These medications are taken orally and alleviate itching, swelling, and hives that result from allergies. The chief side effect of any antihistamine is drowsiness, so the dose should not exceed the recommended amount.

❏ Antiseptics—for cleaning cuts and scrapes. Several antibacterial soaps (pHisoDerm, Betadine, Hibiclens, Dial) are available at drug stores. Hydrogen peroxide can be useful when wounds are especially dirty or when little hands and fingernails pick at scabs or bites. Antibacterial ointments (Polysporin, Bacitracin) can also be used on minor scrapes to reduce the chance of infection. However, ointments containing neomycin, sulfa, or penicillin carry a small risk of sensitization and subsequent allergic reaction. Ask your doctor about them.

❏ Soothing lotions—for skin irritation. Calamine lotion (not Caladryl) is recommended for the initial treatment of itching. Over-the-counter hydrocortisone creams also relieve itching, but since they may have side effects, check with your doctor before beginning treatment. For sunburns or general skin irritations (scuffs, scrapes), unscented moisturizing lotions or aloe vera creams work well. Zinc oxide or other similar ointments (Desitin, vitamin A and D ointment, or Caldesene) are good to have on hand for general chafing.

Some medications need not be included in the home pharmacy even though everyone had them around in the past. For example, aspirin is used less often for children these days because it increases one's tendency to bleed and may be associated with Reye's syndrome, a serious condition that can cause liver damage and neurological deterioration in children with certain viral illnesses such as chicken pox or influenza. For these reasons, aspirin need not be part of your home pharmacy. It still has several very appropriate specific uses—for treating certain forms of arthritis, for example— and so may be used if prescribed by your child's doctor.

Codeine preparations are effective against both pain and coughs, but they are fairly potent medicine and not to be used without a doctor's recommendation and prescription.

We are often asked what kind of cough or decongestant medicine we advise using. In truth, pediatric cough and cold medications are fairly interchangeable and are beneficial only to some patients. Similarly, parents also ask which laxative or antidiarrheal medication to have on hand. Again, we feel such medications need not be part of a general home pharmacy. Most of them are ineffective, and some may even be dangerous.

Above all, please remember to secure *all* medications and ointments safely in a locked box or cabinet. A fishing-tackle box with a lock makes an excellent, portable first-aid kit. In addition to keeping your home medical supplies in one place, it can also be very handy when you travel. Keep a key for it with your car keys. If you're planning an out-of-town trip, we suggest you take along a list of current medications and drug allergies as well as an immunization record. Try, whenever possible, to find out in advance how to reach a doctor and an emergency room with pediatric facilities near your destination.

.   .   .

FIRST-AID KIT

a guide to CPR (cardiopulmonary resuscitation)
adhesive bandages of various shapes and sizes
elastic bandages
Steri-strips
tweezers and scissors
a clean washcloth or paper towels
cotton swabs and cotton balls
a surgical, or other, scrub brush
1-inch and 2-inch Kling rolls; 3-inch gauze pads
nonstick tape splints and a sling
a chemical ice pack that cools when opened
a flashlight and extra batteries
an eye-rinse cup and eye patch
a magnet to remove metal shavings or splinters
a magnifying glass
a thermometer
syrup of ipecac for accidental poison ingestion
acetaminophen (Tylenol, Panadol, Liquiprin) for
    fever and pain
antihistamine (Benedryl) for allergic reactions
antiseptics (pHisoDerm, Betadine, Hibiclens) for cleaning
    cuts and scrapes
soothing lotions or ointments for skin irritations
sunscreen
a bee-sting kit

Another aspect of being prepared is knowing the procedures your doctor's office follows. Discuss with your child's pediatrician, in advance, when and how to call, what to do on weekends and holidays, and when to use the hospital emergency room. Many pediatricians, depending on the facilities available, use the emergency room only for life-threatening problems. In less serious situations, contact your child's doctor first so that he can tell you whether you should go to the emergency room or not. If so, he can notify the personnel on duty and plan for initial care. Drop-in clinics are convenient and have the advantage of "not disturbing the doctor." However, the on-duty physicians or staff may not be experienced in pediatrics and are not likely to be familiar with your child. On the whole, private pediatricians do not favor routine use of emergency drop-in clinics, except in rural communities where the clinic may be much closer than the doctor's office.

Most pediatricians have a system for telephone calls to the office; in our practice we return calls concerning acute illness throughout the day. Others may offer early morning call-in hours during which the doctor is available to talk on the phone. Some doctors have nurses or other personnel who give telephone advice and screen calls. Others discourage the use of the telephone but provide drop-in hours during which no appointment is necessary. Try to use whatever system has been set up. If it is not effective for you, tell the doctor rather than trying to work around it.

You should feel comfortable talking to your doctor; your ability to relate to one another is vital. Sometimes he may tell you that he wishes you had called sooner. At other times he may say that a call seemed unnecessary. You should find a way to tell him when he is not communicating effectively or if he sounds snappy and intimidating. Successful pediatric care depends greatly on frankness, honesty, and trust.

In general, you should feel free to call your doctor at any hour if your child is ill or injured and you need advice or assistance. Pediatricians are often upset to learn that a parent "never calls on weekends," or didn't report a high fever in an infant so as not to "bother" the physician. The doctor may appreciate the parent's consideration but will worry about the day when a serious illness may go unattended because the parent does not wish to "inconvenience" him.

On the other hand, the doctor expects parents to consider his needs and situation as well. Here are some examples of calls that frustrate doctors:

❏ A child has had a sore throat all day. At ten o'clock at night the parent calls asking if the doctor will see the child right away and take a throat culture.

❏ At ten in the morning a parent calls about a fifteen-month-old with a temperature of 104 degrees who seems very ill. When asked to bring the child to the office right away, she tells the receptionist it is more convenient to come at five that afternoon.

❏ A child has had diarrhea for twenty-four hours. The parent calls the doctor at six-thirty a.m. to find out whether the child can go to day care.

These calls are more for the parent's convenience than for the child's benefit, and doctors feel frustrated when problems that could have been attended to during regular hours are brought to their attention much later for no appropriate reason.

It helps to anticipate the possiblity that you might someday wind up visiting an emergency room with your child. A trip to the emergency room may be frightening to your child (and to you!), with all of its noise, bright lights, and intense activity. If your child's condition is not life-threatening—a simple fracture, for example—you may have a long wait while more serious cases are taken care of. Waiting may increase your child's apprehension, so it may help to bring along a cuddly toy or a familiar book. In most situations, you will be able to remain with your child throughout examination and treatment. You can be most effective if you are supportive, calm, and reassuring. If you feel uneasy or don't understand what is happening, ask. Be assertive but not argumentative.

Usually the emergency room doctor can speak with the child's doctor by telephone if necessary. Sometimes your child's pediatrician will be able to meet you at the emergency room, either to provide care or just to offer comfort and assistance. In any case, a follow-up visit to him is usually advisable.

You should fully understand the diagnosis and treatment of your child *before* you leave the emergency room. Because hospital shifts and staff change, it may be difficult later to speak to someone who was there at the time your child was treated. For the same reason, it is important to make sure that you or the child's doctor receives a treatment record from the emergency room.

Thankfully, emergency treatment is rarely necessary. Blessed as they are with underlying health and resilience, children usually get over their ills and injuries with very little medical intervention. A little organization and advance planning will help when more vigorous assistance is required; your preparation will ensure that your child will receive prompt and appropriate treatment. But even when nothing goes wrong—that is, most of the time—you'll rest easier knowing that you're prepared.

Common Childhood Symptoms

*T*his section deals with the symptoms of infections and illnesses that often affect children, such as fevers, sore throats and earaches. Just as we do in daily phone conversations with parents, here we'll try to answer the most common questions parents ask and anticipate the ones they haven't thought of yet.

Because parents hardly ever call to tell us that they suspect their child has, for instance, atypical pneumonia, but rather that he has a bad cough and a fever, we identify problems by their symptoms. Then we explore the possible causes of those symptoms, describe how we distinguish one problem from another, and indicate what is urgent, what requires office or emergency room treatment, and what we can advise as appropriate home intervention. For example, after listing different kinds of headache symptoms (dull, sharp, pounding; with or without fever, nausea, cough), we'll discuss possible causes such as infection, trauma, tension, or allergy. Once you are aware of the possible causes of various symptoms and can begin to distinguish, say, fever headaches from tension headaches, you will feel more confident about your ability to evaluate the necessity for medical intervention.

Fever

Fever, the body's normal response to infection, is often the first signal that a child is sick. The nature of the illness will usually become apparent within three to four days, but when a child first has a fever, parents are faced with agonizing uncertainty: Is it just flu, a cold, a virus, or something more serious? Does it mean pain or just a sleepless night for all? How high will the temperature go?

Although parents may hear over and over again that a high fever does not necessarily mean serious illness, the tendency is to think otherwise, because the higher the temperature, the sicker a child usually looks. He becomes droopy and listless, clings to you, loses his appetite, and looks pathetic. Amidst all of this, remember: **A fever is only a symptom and not an illness in itself.** It is the other symptoms and the child's general appearance and responsiveness that indicate the severity of the illness.

It is important to learn to measure your child's temperature accurately. Hands on the forehead and fever strips generally are not very reliable. Digital thermometers are great for little escape artists but vary in their degree of accuracy. Axillary temperature (taken under the arm) is fairly reliable, but the most reliable way to take a temperature is with a rectal thermometer. An oral thermometer works well for older children who can keep their lips shut tight. Save yourself some trouble by always having extra thermometers on hand.

To take a rectal temperature, put Vaseline on the tip of a rectal thermometer, and while spreading buttocks insert it into the rectum about half an inch. Hold child and thermometer for three minutes. With squirming toddlers this may require two people and a position that pins down the child. Such a mutually unhappy state may be achieved with the child lying either on his back with his knees to his chest, or on his stomach over your lap.

When you take the temperature orally, the thermometer should stay in the *closed* mouth for three minutes. Making certain your little chatterbox remains silent for this time can be a challenge. You might try letting him watch an egg timer. But don't worry. When the temperature is very high, the mercury shoots up quickly, and a minute more or less will not make much difference.

If the thermometer should break, scoop up the mercury onto a folded index card, seal it in two plastic bags, place in an unbreakable container, and discard. Mercury readily vaporizes and should not remain around. It is a toxic substance if inhaled or ingested.

When reading a thermometer, remember that the marks between the numbers stand for tenths of a degree. There is a world of difference between 100.3 degrees and 103 degrees! The advice you get regarding each of these temperatures may differ a great deal, so do read carefully.

We suggest you shake the thermometer down immediately after using it. Wash it off in cool water so that it will be ready next time. In the middle of the night, parents are apt to stick that thermometer in a kid's mouth while they are half asleep. When they see 103 degrees, they may not recall that this was the temperature during the last illness three months ago.

The normal rectal temperature is about 97 to 100.4 degrees Fahrenheit. Oral and axillary temperatures tend to be about a degree lower than rectal temperature. To complicate matters, a temperature is usually a degree higher in the afternoon than in the morning. Most physicians consider a child to have a fever if the rectal temperature is above 100.4 degrees. Low temperatures have no significance unless they occur in a newborn or register less than 94 degrees.

The causes of a fever are indeed numerous and range from the trivial to the life-threatening. A fever can be caused simply by overdressing, for example. Bundling up children in heat-retaining garments can generate "fevers"; and this problem is quickly cured by undressing the child. Teething may sometimes cause a low-grade fever. Since most children usually suffer nothing more than gum pain, pediatricians are wary of dismissing a fever by ascribing it to teething. There will be times, however, when the gums are clearly inflamed, the fever is around 101 degrees, and no other reason can be found for the temperature. If the fever responds to acetaminophen and disappears when the teeth have come in, we may grudgingly admit that teething could have been the cause.

Most often, the cause of a fever is a viral infection, such as a cold, intestinal flu, chicken pox, or any number of other common childhood illnesses. A bacterial infection in the ear, throat, sinuses, lungs, or bladder an also be the source of a fever. Perhaps the most feared cause of fever is meningitis, an inflammation of the membranes that line the brain and spinal cord. Meningitis, which may have either a viral or bacterial origin, is a frightening illness because it can result in damage to the brain or nervous system. Fortunately, it is seldom the cause of a child's fever. Older children with meningitis display classic symptoms: fever, apathy, irritability, severe headaches, and a stiff neck (an inability to nod the head up and down). Infants and toddlers are harder to diagnose. They will be feverish, irritable, and extremely sleepy. In addition, they have a high-pitched cry, and typically the anterior fontanel (the diamond-shaped soft spot in the middle of the baby's skull just above the forehead), will be firm and puffed up. Normally this spot is flat or slightly indented. Occasionally a child with meningitis may have a convulsion.

If meningitis is suspected, the doctor should be called at once. If he also suspects meningitis he will take blood samples and do a spinal tap (lumbar puncture). If meningitis is confirmed, he will hospitalize the child and begin treatment with intravenous antibiotics at once, even though the cause of the inflammation will not be known until the results of a culture of the spinal fluid are learned. If the culture shows no bacteria present, then the cause is probably viral; and since antibiotics don't affect viruses, the treatment will be stopped. Fortunately, viral meningitis usually is not as dangerous as bacterial meningitis. If bacteria are present, then the antibiotic treatment will be continued for ten to twenty-one days. With early diagnosis and prompt treatment, most children recover without the serious complications that make this rare illness so dreaded.

Now that you know some of the causes of a fever, here are some guidelines to help you judge its significance:

❏ Remember that while a fever is the most common sign of illness, it does not necessarily indicate a serious illness.

❏ Evaluate your child's alertness and activity, not just the degree of fever. Some children tend to run higher temperatures than others even though they may have the same illness.

❑   High temperatures, even 106 degrees, are unlikely to cause damage to your child. Indeed, temperatures of 103–105 are actually quite common.

❑   In babies less than three months old, however, temperatures above 101 should be reported to your doctor immediately. In very young infants even little fevers are worrisome.

❑   Pediatricians generally ask to be informed if a baby three to twelve months old has a temperature greater than 103 degrees which persists over several hours despite measures to lower it. They wish to know right away if irritability and unresponsiveness accompany the fever. This is because babies are particularly susceptible to infections of the blood and spinal fluid; such infections tend to generate high fevers.

❑   Children often shiver or tremble when they have a fever. These symptoms are *not* seizures. Seizures (convulsions) may accompany a fever, and they typically occur during the period of rapid rise, not necessarily at the peak of the temperature. One of the most frightening experiences parents can have is watching their infant have a febrile seizure. The child's eyes may roll back or stare expressionlessly, his arms and legs may move in a jerky, rigid, continuous fashion. He may breathe heavily and drool from the side of his mouth; his skin may turn a pale, bluish color. The febrile seizure usually lasts less than a minute, even though the child may appear limp and confused for a few minutes after it subsides.

For all its violence, the typical febrile seizure is not harmful and has no lasting effects other than the parents' frightening memories of the event. During that long minute, hold your child (with his head turned to the side, if possible), stay as calm as possible, and observe his movements and breathing patterns. Once the seizure has subsided, call your doctor to discuss what has occurred and to plan the next step. While it is happening, just try to remember that febrile seizures do not ordinarily harm children; they indicate only that the fever is rising rapidly. In the rare event that the seizure occurs without fever, is prolonged or recurrent, or involves only one part of the body, something more serious may be responsible, and you should notify your doctor immediately.

❏ The most important sign of a serious disease requiring prompt diagnosis and treatment is the *decreasing responsiveness of a child.* Over and over again, we stress the importance of steady and obvious deterioration. If your child is no longer making eye contact, not responding to your voice or touch, not smiling, not making purposeful movements, then the problem may be serious indeed.

❏ Even in the absence of signs of serious illness, a child with an unexplained fever lasting more than three days should be examined. The main reason is to rule out conditions such as a urinary tract infection or ear infection, illnesses that require treatment and can be diagnosed only by an examination.

Sometimes parents undertake the treatment of fever with a passion. There seems to be some deep-rooted feeling that if one can make the fever go away, its cause cannot be very serious. It is easy to forget that fever is only a *sign* of illness and may even serve some function in fighting off infection. Treatment then should be directed only at relieving discomfort—and not at achieving some magic Fahrenheit number. Here are some safe suggestions for treatment:

❑ Dress your child as lightly as possible. Piling on the covers may be a natural response to his feeling cold, but it will raise his body temperature and add to his general discomfort. A little cuddling will often help your child feel less cold (and much more secure) without increasing his temperature.

❑ Encourage him to drink fluids. Small sips taken frequently can do a lot to keep a child hydrated, and cool fluids help decrease body temperature. Children with a temperature can get somewhat dehydrated from sweating and an increased metabolic rate. Dehydration adds to discomfort. Of course, if your child is vomiting, pushing fluids may be both unrealistic and inappropriate.

❑ Give acetaminophen every four hours if the temperature is over 102 or 103 and the child is miserable. (See Table 1 for proper dosage.) However, if your child is sleeping comfortably, there is no need to wake him.

❑ Most pediatric authorities today prefer acetaminophen over aspirin in the treatment of fever, especially if the child has the flu or chicken pox. Aspirin increases the likelihood of bleeding and may be associated with Reye's syndrome, a rare illness that can affect the central nervous system, liver, and other organs. However, if you are advised to use aspirin in a given situation, the dose is generally one *baby* tablet (75 mg) per year of age. On rare occasion, the doctor may prescribe acetaminophen and aspirin together to lower an extremely high temperature.

❑ If the temperature is still 103 or higher a half hour to an hour after appropriate treatment, and the child is still uncomfortable, bathe or sponge him with lukewarm water for fifteen to thirty minutes. *Alcohol rubs should not be used,* since alcohol is absorbed by the skin and may itself lead to convulsions. If bathing still fails to lower the temperature, simply wait until you can repeat the previously described steps.

TABLE 1
Dosage for Acetaminophen

Age	Weight	Drops— 80 mg per 0.8 ml dropperful	Elixir— 160 mg per 5 ml teaspoonful	Chewable 80 mg tablets	Junior-strength 160 mg tablets
to 3 mo.	6–11 lb.	0.4 ml	¼ tsp.	½ tab.	
4–11 mo.	12–17 lb.	0.8 ml	½ tsp.	1 tab.	
12–23 mo.	18–23 lb.	1.2 ml	¾ tsp.	1½ tab.	
2–3 yr.	24–35 lb.		1 tsp.	2 tab.	
4–5 yr.	36–47 lb.		1½ tsp.	3 tab.	
6–8 yr.	48–59 lb.		2 tsp.	4 tab.	2 tab.
9–10 yr.	60–71 lb.		2½ tsp.	5 tab.	2½ tab.

A child over 5 years can have one 325 mg adult tablet, and a child over 10 years can have two adult tablets.

In deciding whether or not to bring your child to the office for an examination, remember that a fever usually breaks during the night. It may, therefore, be low in the morning but return again in the afternoon and peak toward evening. Parents feel relieved when the fever is down, but they may become apprehensive again when it rises after office hours. It's less taxing on everyone if you can bring your child to the office during the day. So even if a fever is not high in the early morning, expect it to go up as the day progresses and plan accordingly!

Headaches

Some parents express surprise when they learn that headaches actually occur in children. It seems that youngsters ought to be free of the tensions and worries that send adults to the bottle of aspirin so often. It turns out that children may have headaches for many reasons, including infection, trauma, eye strain, tension, fatigue, allergies, migraine, (very rarely) tumors or other neurological disorders.

It may be difficult for young children to describe what a headache feels like or explain where it hurts. They may point to their head, ears, eyes, or neck. Some may say it feels funny, heavy, full, noisy (like a drum beating inside their head). Unable to describe what is actually bothering them, they may just act frustrated and cranky.

Pediatricians find it very useful to know just how chronic a headache problem is, how often it occurs, the time of day or night it tends to happen, and how long the headache lasts. Other helpful clues include the intensity and location of pain, its association with activities such as school, reading, sports, or piano lessons, or with exposure to sunlight or allergens.

We encourage parents to treat their child's simple headache with rest and sometimes acetaminophen to counter the pain.

Sudden isolated headaches are often caused by infection or by injury. Infection is especially likely if headache is accompanied by fever. If your child also has muscular aches and pains and loss of appetite, suspect a viral illness such as flu. If a very sore throat is also present, headache may be a symptom of strep infection or viral tonsillitis.

If facial pain or flush is located in the cheeks or is associated with swelling and a purple or dark red discoloration of the eyelid or the skin under the eye, sinusitis, an infection of the lining of the sinus cavities may be the problem. Your child should then be examined by his doctor as soon as possible, because these infections can extend to involve the eye itself.

If a child is alert and able to move his head up and down, meningitis is unlikely, but any child who appears ill, has a fever, headache, a stiff neck on downward motion, or a fullness of the fontanel (the soft spot on top of the head), should be examined at once to determine if meningitis or another infection is present.

Head and neck injuries (trauma) resulting from falls or other accidents can lead to an acute, severe headache over the traumatized area or anywhere else on the head or neck. Pediatricians continue to await the birth of a helmet so appealing that children will actually wear it on bicycles, skateboards, roller skates, and other forms of rapid transit. Until that day comes, we hound our young patients to wear the helmets available, and we suggest you do the same.

Because the brain is enclosed in the skull, sudden motion with impact can jar the tissues (concussion) or bruise them (contusion). Concussion causes headache, sometimes together with loss of consciousness, nausea, vomiting, and drowsiness. Symptoms of concussion should be reported to your doctor, who will then determine whether he should see the child and give you specific instructions about what you should watch for and report to him.

Parents often attribute frequent headaches to eye strain. It turns out that it is a relatively rare cause of headaches in children. Most vision problems are identified by annual eye examinations or because signs of difficulty seeing have become obvious. When eyes are checked as a cause of chronic headaches, the results are usually negative.

All too often, in today's world, the cause of headaches turns out to be tension. These headaches can be felt anywhere on the head and neck but are most often associated with tightness in the back of the scalp. The pain can be dull and nagging, or sharp and throbbing. Muscles of the neck sometimes feel hard because they are in spasm.

At what age can children have tension-related headaches? Alas, even toddlers can experience emotional strain. Imagine a rushed breakfast, in and out of the car seat, a few sirens, perhaps a sudden stop, being left at day care, a bite and a shove, all occurring one after the other. Many older children also lead relatively hectic lives filled with academic, social, and family pressures. Special circumstances, such as long parental absences, prolonged travel, or other uprooting experiences may add to the tension. Some children feel they must excell in sports or dance. These special activities bring benefits, but can also lead to headaches or other manifestations of overload.

It is therefore useful to explore areas of potential tension when trying to figure out the cause of recurring headaches. Encourage children to talk about their problems and pay attention when they do. An attempt to identify possible areas of stress and to modify pressures will often help a child with tension or fatigue headaches. It may be useful to establish rituals with young children, such as routinely having them mention the best and worst event of their day. Older children are frequently less direct and take their clues from how their parents express their own worries. It is important to be accessible to older children so that they can talk about their problems at the odd moments when they choose to do so. Although rest, massage, and pain medication can relieve a tension headache, a better solution to the problem is to get at its root.

Headache may also be one of many manifestations of allergy. Histamine, the primary chemical released in allergic reactions, can cause headaches. Nasal congestion can aggravate a sense of fullness around the nose and forehead, and the sinuses can be congested if they are developed. The best treatment for this type of headache is treatment of the underlying allergy by avoiding the irritant. If this is not feasible, an antihistamine medication may relieve the headache symptoms, at least temporarily.

Migraine-type or vascular headaches are more common in childhood than we used to think. These headaches often run in families and may have a similar age of onset over several generations. They are often felt as pounding over the temples and may be preceded by visual disturbances, sensitivity to light, watery eyes, and numbness or unusual sensations in the arms and fingers. They may also be accompanied by nausea, vomiting, or abdominal pain. Simple pain medication and ice packs may be sufficient treatment. If so, we suggest keeping a few ice-pack gels in the freezer, since the onset of migraine headaches can be sudden and unexpected. Where simple measures do not work, other medications that specifically treat vascular headaches may be appropriate.

Physical exertion, heat, and exposure to sun or wind are less common causes of headaches. Sometimes a child diagnoses himself when he tells you he only gets headaches if he has been playing ball without his hat. Sunglasses, hats with shady brims, and extra fluids can also help prevent these headaches. Some perfectly healthy children need to rest during exercise, but if exertion seems a common circumstance associated with headache symptoms, elevated blood pressure should be considered; in any event, any examination for headache should include a check of the blood pressure.

Neurological diseases or brain tumors are the least

likely causes of chronic headaches. The dread of a brain tumor, however, leads almost everyone to think about the possibility when headaches are frequent. The headache caused by tumor is characteristically most severe on arising in the morning. Headaches increase in frequency and intensity and are accompanied by recurrent vomiting. Later, additional neuromuscular symptoms, such as weakness of the arms and legs or loss of balance may be noticed. Additional symptoms include seizures, changes in vision such as blurred or double vision, significant unexplained hearing loss, or a noticeably impaired ability to think or speak as usual. Any child with a suspected neurological disorder should be examined promptly by his doctor.

Fortunately, the causes of most headaches are minor, and the symptoms respond well to home treatment. Simple headaches may serve as protective warning devices that tell us something is too taxing, too nerve-racking, or too irritating for our own good.

Earaches

Some children seem to have an earache just about all the time. In their frustration, parents try to prevent earaches and catch them before they create havoc in the middle of the night. Hoping they are neither too early nor too late, parents try to figure out just when to call the doctor and have their child's ears checked out. It's not an easy task; sometimes even we pediatricians, who are looking at the eardrum with years of training and experience, cannot be certain whether an ear infection is or is not brewing.

We are asked many questions about the vexing problem of recurrent ear infections: Should I suspect an ear infection if my child starts saying "what?" all the time? Won't there be pain and fever if there is an infection? Does swimming or bath water in the ears cause ear infections? Will covering the ears in cold weather help prevent infections? Does treating a cold with decongestants prevent them? Is day care a factor? Will flying cause earache, ear infection, or damage to the eardrum?

To answer these questions, it helps to know a little bit about the ear. Most earaches are the result of bacterial or viral infections of the middle ear. Other less common causes include any process that distorts the shape of the eardrum, altitude change, referred pain from teething, and inflammation of the external ear canal. The middle ear chamber is separated from the outside world by the eardrum. Therefore, as long as the eardrum is intact, cold weather, wind, and water will not affect anything that happens in the middle ear. Hats, scarves, and earmuffs offer no protection whatsoever!

The middle ear drains into the throat through the eustachian tube, which is not only smaller in infants than in adults, but is also relatively more horizontal. For this reason, young children are anatomically more prone to poor ear drainage than older ones. Fluid that settles in the middle ear space and fails to drain is a perfect home for bacteria. If accumulating fluid places pressure on the eardrum, pain results.

Any condition that causes swelling of the tissues in the nose and throat tends to slow down or block middle ear drainage as well. This is how colds, nasal allergy, or chemical irritation can contribute to the likelihood of ear infection. A vacuum caused by sudden pressure change can collapse the tiny eustachian tube and suck in the eardrum. The body reacts to this vacuum by secreting fluid in the middle ear. This reaction explains why a plane ride, especially one compounded by an ongoing cold, can lead to an ear infection. Since the greatest pressure change occurs during takeoff and landing, nursing or other chewing activity during this time can reduce the chance of a vacuum effect in the middle ear.

Finally, poor eustachian-tube function can be an inherited trait, making some children more prone to infection from any cause. This fact may help explain why only some children in a group get recurrent ear infections while others seem to sail through without problems. On the whole, however, when infection is the cause, the presence of young siblings, day-care exposures, and crowded living situations do make the recurrence of ear infection more likely.

Ear infections have a wide range of symptoms. In infants, fever, inconsolable crying, irritability, diminished appetite, vomiting, poking or scratching the ear, and night waking may all be signs of ear pain. Toddlers may also shake their heads or point to the inside of their mouths. Older children should be able to tell you but may misinterpret the location of their pain. They may say their mouth or jaw hurts, shake their head, or hold their forehead.

Most commonly, ear infections occur at the tail end of a cold, when everything ought to be getting better. In fact, if a cold persists beyond ten to fourteen days, especially in a child who cannot talk yet, suspect an ear infection and consider having his ears examined to rule out the possibility of ear infection.

Symptoms may also vary depending on the location of the infection and on the presence of pus and inflammation. Infection of the external ear, the canal between the earlobe and the eardrum, results in pain when the earlobe is moved. A white or clear discharge may occasionally be seen. The most common type of *external otitis* is swimmer's ear. Recurrent exposure to water may injure the delicate lining of the ear canal, allowing bacteria or fungal organisms to breed.

Children who spend a lot of time in the water may occasionally develop external otitis if measures are not taken to dry the ear canal. Try drawing the water off with the corner of a towel; or use 4 to 6 drops of a half-and-half solution of vinegar and alcohol.

Another cause of ear inflammation is mechanical injury caused by cuts or puncture wounds. You should discourage your children from sticking any object into their ears. Nothing sharp or penetrating should ever be put into the ear. Don't clean inside the ear with cotton swabs or anything else! Avoiding injury challenges even the doctor when he cleans out ear wax.

Doctors distinguish three conditions involving the middle ear that can lead to earache or disturbed hearing. Fluid in the middle ear is termed *serous otitis,* fluid with inflammation is termed *serous otitis with effusion,* and the same with signs of pus formation and pressure on the eardrum is termed *otitis media.* If the pressure is great enough, the eardrum may rupture (perforate), and pus may run out of the ear.

In serous otitis, the pain is typically fleeting. Other signs are loud speech, decreased hearing, peculiar popping or ringing sounds in the ear, and loss of balance. Serous otitis is often associated with colds or allergies. It is usually a benign and self-limiting condition that causes trouble only if it leads to infection or to persistent diminished hearing.

Otitis media, because of the presence of pus under pressure, is more commonly associated with severe, throbbing, unremitting pain in the ear and fever, irritability, and, occasionally, vomiting. However, it is entirely possible to have well-established otitis media *without* pain or other outward signs. Also, the sudden end of pain may be due to perforation of the eardrum and should not lead you away from the suspicion of ear infection if fever and other signs persist or if the ear starts to drain.

The severity of pain is not a very reliable index of the seriousness of ear infections. Some children seem to have extraordinarily high pain thresholds, while others are extremely sensitive. But earache always deserves respect and attention.

Antibiotics are most important to eradicate ear infection, but they will do nothing for pain in the middle of the night because they do not start to take effect for six to eight hours. But there are things *you* can do while waiting for the doctor's office and the pharmacy to open. The first is to give the child an analgesic (pain killer) such as acetaminophen. If your child is prone to frequent earaches, your doctor may prescribe a stronger pain medication for you to keep on hand. External warmth applied with a hot water bottle or a heating pad set on low may soothe the pain. One or two drops of an anesthetic preparation (such as Auralgan) or warm olive oil every two to four hours may also help relieve the pain. Nothing, however, should be placed in the ear if there is drainage suggesting possible rupture of the eardrum.

Decongestant/antihistamines may be useful if ear pain is caused by pressure changes alone. In this case, these medications may dry mucus or reduce tissue swelling sufficiently to eliminate pain, but they do not seem to prevent ear infections.

It is important that a child with suspected ear infection be examined to establish the diagnosis. If it turns out to be external otitis, antibiotic drops may be prescribed. If it is serous otitis, the doctor may choose to watch without treatment. If there is an effusion or otitis media, most pediatricians will prescribe oral antibiotics.

The aim of antibiotic treatment is to destroy bacteria, prevent complications of untreated infection, and secondarily, to reduce pain. This is often easier said than done, because antibiotics do not readily enter the middle ear space.

The treatment will not work if the infection is caused by a virus or if the bacteria are relatively resistant to the chosen antibiotic. The only way to tell in advance which antibiotic to use is to analyze fluid drawn from the eardrum with a needle. Most pediatricians consider this procedure both impractical and incompatible with any ongoing relationship with the patient! How do doctors choose which antibiotic to use? Sometimes our choice is influenced by what seems to be working in the community. Sometimes, if the patient is finicky, taste is important. Sometimes potential side effects influence our choice.

All too often, if ear infections recur, they do not respond as well to antibiotic treatment. This is not because the body becomes "immune" to the antibiotic, but because the few remaining bugs tend to be the hardier, more resistant ones. Doctors therefore try not to use antibiotics except when really necessary.

Because of the possibility of resistance, and because chronic serous otitis may follow an acute infection, pediatricians generally ask to see the patient again after ten to fourteen days of antibiotic therapy. If the infection has not cleared, the treatment may be extended, or another antibiotic may be tried. It is very important to *complete the full course of antibiotics* in order to eradicate the bacteria. It is also important to *return after the treatment is completed* to have the ear reexamined. Fluid behind the eardrum, as well as smoldering infection may persist without symptoms. If months go by, the problem of retained middle ear fluid can distort hearing and eventually affect language.

If ear infections recur consistently, or if serous otitis perists beyond three to four months to the point of potential hearing impairment, long-term prophylactic antibiotics or a search for allergic conditions may be tried. If this fails, your child's doctor may recommend that ventilation tubes be placed in the eardrums. In this relatively minor operation, performed by an ear-nose-and-throat surgeon, a small plastic tube shaped like a doughnut is placed onto the eardrum to provide drainage. Afterward, infections can usually be treated with ear drops alone.

So there you have the earache—painful, troublesome, and all too common.

Sore Throats

A child old enough to talk can probably *tell* you when he has a sore throat. But a very young child who can't yet say exactly what's bothering him presents a real challenge to parents. If your child is drooling a bit, cranky, refusing to eat, and has a fever, it probably is a sore throat.

There are many causes of sore throat, ranging from a dry sensation in the throat, often from mouth breathing, to irritating mucus drainage to infection. The lymph nodes in the neck generally function to filter and process bacteria and viruses entering the respiratory passages; and a pair of guardians in particular, namely the tonsils, seem to get an undue share of the onslaught. Tonsillitis may be caused by viruses or by bacteria. The viral varieties of tonsillitis are often associated with colds; bacterial infections may be due to any of several organisms. (See chapter on infections.)

Sometimes throat cultures reveal bacteria that may be normal residents of the mouth or nose, and the doctor must decide whether these are to be treated or not. Most pediatricians agree that a streptococcal (strep) infection requires treatment, because it can lead to severe complications that may affect the heart (rheumatic fever) or the kidneys (glomerulonephritis).

During some epidemics, doctors can often diagnose strep throat from the appearance of the throat alone, but to be certain, a culture should be taken. Don't try do-it-yourself diagnosis. For instance, the presence of small white spots on the tonsils is not very specific for strep infections; the same spots appear in viral tonsillitis. In older children, mononucleosis should also be suspected as a possible cause of severe sore throat and tonsillitis.

"Scarlet fever" is a term used to describe strep throat with fever and a characteristic rash. The throat is usually very sore and red, sometimes several days before the rash appears. The skin becomes red and rough, especially over the chest. The area around the lips often remains pale. The tongue takes on the appearance of a red strawberry.

The treatment for both strep throat and scarlet fever is a ten-day course of oral antibiotics (penicillin, erythromycin). Children are considered no longer contagious forty-eight hours after antibiotics have been initiated. Strep throat sometimes recurs despite adequate treatment, and a second course of therapy with the same antibiotic (or a different one) is usually prescribed. Some doctors treat strep with antibiotic injections, but on the whole, oral medications do the trick.

What about removing tonsils? It used to be done much more commonly than it is now. In general, we suggest tonsillectomy only in a few situations: When bacterial tonsillitis recurs often enough to cause many school absences, or when chronic tonsillitis is cured by neither time nor antibiotics, removal may be the best solution. It may also be called for when the tonsils swell enough to interfere with breathing, especially at night.

Be aware, however, that tonsils have a growth pattern of their own: They are quite large in children from about age three to six. Then during late childhood and early adolescence, the tonsils shrink. Appearance alone, therefore, is not a good criterion. If you notice restless sleeping patterns, hear snoring and chortling sounds during the night, and observe your child taking unusually deep breaths while asleep, all in the presence of enlarged tonsils, report these signs to the doctor. We might perform x-rays first to determine the size of the adenoids, also lymph-node tissue—similar to the tonsils, but situated at the back of the nose. Occasionally the adenoids, the tonsils, or both might need to go.

Adenoidectomy is a relatively minor procedure involving brief anesthesia and very short recovery time. Tonsillectomy, on the other hand, is more involved and may entail some bleeding as well as more and longer discomfort.

The simple discomfort of sore throat can be treated by a variety of measures: If your child is able to gargle, from age eight or so, you can mix ½ teaspoon of salt with six to eight ounces of water and create a soothing saline solution to use several times a day as needed. A three percent solution of hydrogen peroxide mixed with an equal amount of water or any commercial soothing gargle can be used in the same way. Some children benefit from sucking on a honey drop or lozenge, but the child needs to be old enough to ensure that choking will not be a problem (six or older). Tea-and-honey concoctions are useful, but cannot be given to children less than a year of age because of the risk of infant botulism, a paralyzing illness due to bacteria that like to live in honey. Acetaminophen may help reduce pain. Breast-fed infants will wish to nurse more often; older children may find some solace in ice cream, milk shakes, and Popsicles.

Coughs

Telephone sleuths—that's how we often see ourselves as we listen to parents' descriptions of their child's cough and try to figure out what the problem might be. "What does the cough sound like?" the pediatrician asks. "Like there's a barking seal in the crib." "Like there's a whistling teapot in the bedroom." "A honk." "It's dry and hacking." "There's a rattle deep in the chest." Based on these vivid descriptions, we need to decide whether the child's cough requires treatment or not.

It surprises many parents that we often see a cough as a bit of a friend. A cough is the body's natural response to irritation in the respiratory tract (when the irritation is in the nose, mouth, or throat, we call it upper-airway irritation; lower-airway irritation is in the bronchi or lungs). In and of itself, a cough does not imply serious illness. In fact, like sneezing, it is a protective mechanism—the body's way of cleaning excess mucus from the bronchi or lungs. Sometimes a cough is startlingly forceful and produces a lot of mucus, which is then swallowed. At times children vomit after coughing, but mostly they swallow the mucus and it may appear in their stool.

There are many causes of simple coughs. For example, they may be caused by environmental irritations, such as smoke, or by allergies—say, to cat fur or to mold. Dry air, or dust, paint, fumes, pollen, and other common substances may also irritate the lining of the nose and throat, causing coughing and sneezing. A sore throat may also cause a cough.

We get seriously concerned about a cough only when it is severe enough to interfere with eating and sleeping, and when it is accompanied by signs of labored, rapid breathing or by symptoms of more serious illness such as bronchitis or asthma. Some physical clues that indicate the body is working harder than normal to bring air into the lungs are flaring of the nostrils and the use of so-called accessory muscles of respiration, which results in the visible contraction of the muscles of the neck and those above, between, and below the ribs. Other signs of breathing stress include rapid, shallow breaths, crowing sounds (stridor) while inhaling, or whistling sounds (wheezing) while exhaling. (Let us quickly add that rapid breathing often accompanies fever, and, by itself, need not be looked upon as a sign of breathing difficulty when fever is present.)

Children naturally become extremely agitated and anxious when they are having difficulty breathing. Try to be calm and reassuring yourself; if you panic, it will make your child even more panicky. In extreme situations, blue lips or nails indicate that not enough oxygen is reaching the blood; in that case, something needs to be done fast. This is fortunately quite rare, but if it happens, call your doctor at once.

What should you do at home about a simple cough, one not associated with any·of the signs of trouble listed above? Most coughs that are not interfering with sleeping or eating do not require medication, and simple practical measures are all you need. Keeping mucus as thin as possible may be helpful, and the best way to accomplish this is to encourage your child to drink fluids. A child may benefit from propping up the head of his bed. A baby can be placed in an infant seat —set on the floor or secured in the crib—or the crib mattress can be elevated slightly with blocks or books. A humidifier, a vaporizer, or pans of water placed near the heater may help if the cough is due to irritation from dry air.

Many cold and cough medicines line the counters of drugstores. To dry up mucus or to counter simple coughs, a variety of over-the-counter or prescription decongestant and antihistamine preparations, with or without expectorants and cough suppressants, are available. There are some differences among them, but by and large, they are fairly interchangeable. Any age-appropriate pediatric preparation is likely to be tolerated by a child who weighs more than eighteen to twenty pounds. Some of these preparations make children drowsy or make them irritable or jumpy. Doses are determined by weight, unless indicated by age on the bottle. We feel that the promotional claims made for these medications are mostly overstated, and we do not prescribe them routinely.

In certain circumstances, especially when a cough is depriving a child of sleep, a specific cough suppressant may be prescribed by your child's doctor. The most effective cough suppressants are codeine and its chemical analogs. Because of codeine's addictive potential and because we do not wish to lose the useful side of coughing, we prescribe it and other cough suppressants most judiciously.

Further measures to treat cough depend on its severity and specific cause. For example, if the cough comes from a sore throat, tea with honey, honey drops, or lozenges are generally appropriate for children six years and older. Infants under a year of age cannot be given honey because it carries a risk of infant botulism, a paralyzing illness.

Croup, the childhood equivalent of laryngitis, is easy to recognize. With its peculiar barking cough and sudden late-night onset, croup may seem quite frightening at first. The symptoms of croup include fast, labored breathing, exaggerated chest motion with each breath, the barking cough, and a characteristic crowing sound when the child takes a breath. As long as your child is breathing comfortably, even if he is making these sounds, the chances are very good that the problem is not too serious. On the other hand, the opening through the larynx (voicebox) and trachea (windpipe) that allows the passage of air is quite narrow in children, especially those under the age of five. There can be serious trouble if it begins to close off, but fortunately this is very rare, and that horrible sound of croup is generally easy to control.

Home treatment consists of one or more trips to a hot, steamy bathroom, where the child breathes moist air for ten to twenty minutes until the croup improves. Sometimes croup is further relieved by taking the child outside, especially if the air is moist or humid.

This common kind of croup, usually due to a virus, lasts for three or four days, may have some associated fever, and is typically worse at night and better during the day. A child prone to croup may have repeated episodes, until his larynx and trachea have grown enough to eliminate those symptoms.

With severe croup, the exceptional variety that may be bacterial in origin, the picture is different: The child looks ill, usually runs a high fever, has labored breathing, asks to sit up, holds his head still, and drools. If you begin to see these symptoms, your child may have a particularly serious form of croup called epiglottitis that warrants an immediate call to the doctor and prompt treatment in the emergency room.

The symptoms of croup can also be caused by choking if an object is lodged in the throat or windpipe. It helps if parents are always alert to the possibility that their child might have "swallowed" something that went down the wrong way. Foreign bodies are often easier to retrieve when they first lodge.

The cough of asthma is usually associated with wheezing, a whistling sound heard when the child exhales. Asthma (recurrent episodes of wheezing) occurs when something irritates the lower airway or lungs. Some children develop asthma because their lungs react to an allergen such as pollen, or to an environmental or infectious agent. If you suspect that allergy is the cause, the irritant should be removed if at all possible. For example, a child who wheezes in the presence of feathers should not have a bird for a pet or sleep on a down pillow. When it is not possible to avoid the irritant, your child's doctor may prescribe one of several medications called bronchodilators—which may be given by inhaler, tablet, syrup, or injection—to undo the constriction in the air passages. At times, additional medications such as cromolyn sodium or cortisone preparations are necessary to prevent or treat severe asthma. If wheezing leads to breathing that is labored or rapid (faster than forty or fifty breaths a minute), or if it impairs your child's ability to speak easily or to drink, it is time to call your doctor. Although most episodes of asthma can be treated at home or in the doctor's office, in some circumstances, emergency-room treatment or hospitalization becomes necessary.

However, all wheezing is not due to asthma. Wheezing results from plugging or constriction at the end of the air passages to the lungs. Some children wheeze periodically with respiratory infections during the first years of life, but not later. Wheezing can also occur if a foreign body, such as a peanut or a bead, lodges in the air passages. Parents need to be alert to this possibility, since symptoms may subside for a while, only to turn up again later, when everyone has forgotten the first symptoms of gagging and coughing.

The cough of bronchitis may be particularly deep, hacking, and frequent. It usually disrupts sleep, may result in vomiting, and can make it difficult for a child to eat. Consult your doctor if you think your child has bronchitis. Sometimes, treatment will be confined to simple measures against the cough. If your child is also wheezing, though, specific bronchodilator medication may be appropriate. Most bronchitis is due to a virus, for which there is no specific treatment; but some doctors will prescribe an antibiotic if they suspect the bronchitis is caused by bacteria.

The same symptoms can also be caused by pneumonia, a deeper inflammation involving lung tissue itself. The word *pneumonia* strikes fear into the hearts of many parents; indeed, it was once one of the most serious childhood illnesses. But not today! Children with pneumonia usually respond promptly to treatment and do very well. Unless it recurs frequently, pneumonia does not imply any problem with immunity or resistance. Contrary to popular belief, pneumonia is not the result of a neglected cold that has descended into the lungs. Pneumonia typically results when a virus or bacteria "selects" the lungs as its home. The seriousness and extent of the disease often depend on the age and general health of the child. The diagnosis may even come as a complete surprise to parents, because the symptoms can be relatively mild, and the child may be up and around and not appear very ill.

A deep, hacking cough, combined with fever, labored breathing, and chest or abdominal pain, may mean pneumonia. The child's doctor determines whether or not the lungs are involved by listening to the sound of breathing with a stethoscope. He may wish to confirm his clinical diagnosis with a chest x-ray, or to find out more about the nature of the illness through some blood tests. If he thinks the pneumonia is caused by bacteria, he may prescribe antibiotics.

If your child is coughing so much at night that he cannot sleep, your doctor may also prescribe a cough suppressant. Certainly you may give your child acetaminophen or a lukewarm bath to lower his temperature. But no additional restrictions are needed. Most youngsters will regulate their own activity and rest if they are exhausted or too weak to run about. Children can usually return to school two or three days after beginning treatment for pneumonia.

. . .

We are often asked whether children can "catch a cough" from one another. It is certainly possible to pass germs in this fashion, but only while the virus or bacteria are present. The contagious period varies for each illness, but generally includes only a few days before and the first days after the onset of the actual illness. A cough caused by excess mucus, allergy, or irritation is not contagious at all.

Whatever the cause, a cough may persist for several weeks after a child otherwise seems well. Although it is often difficult to wait for a cough to disappear without treatment, it is generally safe to do so as long as your child has no other sign of increasing illness and is eating and sleeping well. When evaluating your child's cough, think of the whole child, not just that nagging sound he is making. Your anxiety about a cough may diminish when you see before you a child who can beat you around the track without effort and empty your refrigerator at a moment's notice, even if he is *still* coughing.

Vomiting

Vomiting is common in children. It's messy, but usually not dangerous. Some children vomit often; others hardly ever do so. Some children vomit when they are frightened or emotionally upset. Others vomit when they have a variety of illnesses, such as ear infection or flu.

Vomiting is most often a result of intestinal flu or a sign of food intolerance, but it can be a symptom of a more serious abdominal problem, such as bowel obstruction or appendicitis. It can also accompany problems originating outside the abdomen, such as concussion or kidney infection. When this is the case, the clue comes from other symptoms that accompany the vomiting, such as rapid breathing and fever.

Children tend to vomit forcefully and repeatedly, and parents may feel helpless as they try to comfort a child who is panicked by his inability to control what is happening to him. Worried that their child may become dehydrated, parents lovingly encourage him to drink fluids even before his stomach has had a chance to settle down. But take heart: most healthy children do not get dehydrated from throwing up, especially as they grow older. If you are aware of the signs of dehydration, and if you can recognize the few situations when vomiting may indicate something more serious than simple flu or minor food intolerance, you can effectively care for your child at home. The methods are simple; the patience and stamina needed can be harder to find.

All infants spit up to some degree because of the relative immaturity of their esophagus and stomach. Even so, babies usually gain weight just fine and stop spitting up between four to six months of age. A few have exaggerated spitting up or continue it longer, say until ten months. This condition is called gastrointestinal reflux. Sometimes it is eased by propping the baby in a sitting position after feeding or by thickening his formula, if he is receiving one. Rarely, medication is required if the problem is particularly vexing.

In general, vomiting is distinguished from spitting up by the larger volume of the material brought up. A particular kind of vomiting, called projectile vomiting, results when there is a constriction at the lower end of the stomach, a condition called pyloric stenosis. Projectile vomiting shoots across the room several feet and typically contains food the child has just eaten. Once the vomiting has stopped, he is likely to appear happy and hungry again. If the condition goes untreated and vomiting continues, the child is likely to lose weight. Pyloric stenosis is usually diagnosed by x-ray and the narrowing can be corrected by surgery.

Another important, though rare, cause of vomiting is

bowel obstruction. It can occur at any age and at any level of the intestines as a result of anatomic abnormalities. An obstruction causes the bile to back up into the stomach, staining the vomit bright green. (Dry heaves, which may produce a little fluid that isn't green, are more associated with simple flu or food intolerance.) As a bowel obstruction persists, the abdomen typically becomes distended and is painful when touched. If your child shows these signs of obstruction, notify your doctor at once; it is vital that the obstruction be relieved as soon as possible.

The main signs, then, that vomiting could be serious include projectile vomiting, bile-stained green vomit, and distension of the abdomen. Also important are associated signs of intestinal inflammation suggesting appendicitis (see Abdominal Pain) or signs of other serious illness outside the abdomen. Small amounts of blood in the vomit are common, especially after forceful vomiting, but if the vomit contains a considerable amount of bright red blood or material that looks like coffee grounds (digested blood), you should notify your doctor; these signs could indicate an ulcer.

If you see none of these symptoms, you can care for your child at home. Treatment of a child who is vomiting requires patience, sympathy, and perseverence. Whatever you do, be sure to increase fluids *slowly,* even if your child is thirsty. Vomiting can be very frightening to a young child, and comfort and reassurance are equally important. The two principles in the treatment of vomiting are: (1) allow the irritated stomach and intestines to rest after emptying, and (2) limit feeding to frequent small amounts of clear liquids.

1. Never feed your child while he is actively vomiting. Wait at least an hour after he has stopped vomiting—even if he is thirsty—before offering him anything to drink.

Wait even longer if he is not interested in drinking. During this time, a small quantity of ice chips may be given to older children to relieve thirst.

2.   When your child seems ready, you can offer small amounts of clear fluid, such as a few tablespoons of flat cola or other soda (pour it and let it stand until it no longer fizzes), cola syrup diluted with water, an electrolyte solution made especially for infants (Pedialyte, Infalyte, etc.), or runners' electrolyte solution (for older children). Then wait twenty to thirty minutes. If there is no further vomiting, you can slowly increase the *amount* of fluid, while maintaining the same *interval* between drinks. But be careful to increase the amount of fluids *slowly,* even if your child seems thirsty and impatient.

Once clear fluids are tolerated in unlimited amounts, babies may resume breast or formula feedings. Older children may be able to eat Popsicles or Jell-O. After twenty-four hours without vomiting, a child may progress to light solid foods, such as crackers, toast, and perhaps a soft-boiled egg. If the stomach is overwhelmed at any point, vomiting will resume. You then will have to go back to offering clear fluids, starting with an even smaller amount and progressing at an even slower pace, with a half hour rest between feedings. A child who has been vomiting may go for days with no recurrence, and just when you think it is all over, have another spell of vomiting. Stomach and intestines take time to get back to normal and are easily irritated, so keep a basin and towels close at hand.

If your child fails to respond to simple home treatment after six to eight hours (and even sooner in infants), his condition should be reported to your doctor. The primary concern is the possibility of dehydration. When the amount of fluid lost through vomiting or diarrhea exceeds the body's ability to replace it, dehydration results.

Fortunately, dehydration is relatively rare, especially as your child grows older, larger, and heavier. Early signs of dehydration include dry skin, absence of tears, reduced urine output, and sunken soft spot (fontanel) in infants. Further dehydration may result in shriveled skin (resembling a prune's) and lack of urine production. We get concerned if the child doesn't urinate for eight hours. Sometimes children in this situation require some intravenous fluids to get them back on the right track. Some medications, given as suppositories, may help reduce the urge to vomit, but most doctors will consider giving such medication only after they have examined the child and excluded a more serious illness. If the vomiting cannot be controlled at home, the child will be treated in the emergency room or admitted to the hospital for intravenous rehydration. This allows stomach and intestines to rest, and within a day or two, the child is usually running around the ward, clamoring to go home and play.

Periodic vomiting often disappears after a while, with no cause having been found. Rarely, it is due to an anatomic problem, but recurrent vomiting can also arise in disturbed or emotionally upset children. Occasionally we see children with recurrent vomiting, sometimes self-induced. If vomiting is frequent, self-induced, or associated with weight loss, your pediatrician should be consulted.

Finally, a comment about motion sickness. This is a tough one! Some children are just very sensitive to motion and easily become nauseated, especially if they are in the back of the car with the windows closed. We suggest planning routes that are as straight as possible, frequent stops, and open windows whenever possible. Medications are available to counter motion sickness, but these are quite variable in their effectiveness.

Considering all the situations in which a child may vomit, it's amazing that no one has yet invented the disposable, designer, fold-out basin! Who knows: perhaps it's on the drawing board somewhere.

Abdominal Pain

When a child says, "My tummy hurts," parents often think, "Maybe it's appendicitis." Remembering something about the right lower abdomen, they are apt to ask their child to point to the spot that hurts. But whatever the cause of abdominal pain, most children seem to feel it most right around their belly button. So that is where they almost always point, and you, the parent, remain perplexed!

What causes abdominal pain? So much seems hidden inside the abdomen that pain there appears particularly mysterious and distressing, especially when cramps are severe enough to cause crying. Because the pain can be so intense, parents are likely to conclude that the problem must be serious. Although you should be alert to that possibility, you should also be reassured that abdominal pain is common in children and usually does not signify an emergency.

In fact, many times, the cause of a belly ache lies outside the abdomen entirely. Many illnesses such as pneumonia or an ear infection can cause the intestines to move abnormally. Abdominal pain may be the reason a child goes to the doctor, but his illness may turn out not to be in the abdomen at all.

When the pain is abdominal in cause, two signs will help you distinguish an urgent problem: *abdominal rigidity* and *rebound tenderness*. The first term describes marked resistance you may feel when you gently push on the abdomen with your hand. The second refers to the abdominal pain that the child describes when you suddenly let go after having gently pushed in with your hand. If one or both of these signs are present, it is time to call your doctor. They could indicate severe inflammation of the intestines and the lining of the abdominal cavity.

Persistent pain that begins around the navel and then settles in the right side of the abdomen below the navel is typically the first sign of appendicitis. (Very occasionally the appendix is not in its usual location and the pain may be felt elsewhere.) Over the next few hours, the pain increases in intensity, the abdomen feels rigid when pressed, and there may be rebound tenderness. A low-grade fever of 100 to 102 degrees, accompanied by nausea or mild vomiting, often occurs after the pain begins. A child with appendicitis is not anxious to jump around, and he walks as if his abdomen hurts. The symptoms are quite unlike those of intestinal flu. A child with intestinal flu usually vomits and has a fever before he complains of abdominal pain, and his pain is crampy and much more diffuse. In the case of an ordinary belly ache caused by flu or gas, a small amount of resistance to hand pressure may be encountered, but it is usually possible to push against the abdomen without causing marked discomfort if you do it gently while distracting your child with a joke or a story. And when you let go, the pain become less rather than more intense.

A child with appendicitis will be admitted to the hospital and surgery will be performed to remove the appendix. It is important that this be done without delay because if the appendix ruptures, a more serious condition known as peritonitis, an infection and inflammation of the intestines, may result. This condition complicates surgery and may require a course of antibiotics and abdominal drainage. The normal hospital stay for a simple appendectomy is three to four days. If the appendix ruptures, however, a child may need to remain in the hospital a few extra days.

A sign of another potentially urgent problem, obstructed bowel, is stomach pain accompanied by bile-stained vomiting. Bile is bright green in color, and its presence, especially together with a distended belly, could mean an obstructed bowel. If the vomit is green, you should call the doctor promptly.

A second sign of a bowel obstruction is a crampy abdominal pain that comes and goes. Cramps tend to come in waves and in between, the child may smile and show interest in a story or a television program. When the problem is serious, these periods of relief become increasingly brief or may disappear altogether. This pain is distinguished from that of simple intestinal flu by progressively severe discomfort, green vomiting, absence of bowel movements, and the pale, sick appearance of the child.

One form of bowel obstruction that most commonly occurs in children between the ages of four months and two years is intussusception. It is especially important to diagnose this condition early, because if it goes unrecognized the bowel can be injured and surgery will be necessary. Intussusception is a telescoping of the bowel that causes the intestinal wall to fold in on itself, leading to swelling, disruption of the blood supply, and intestinal blockage. A child with intussusception becomes pale and very quiet and will have an expression of severe pain on his face. Abdominal rigidity, rebound tenderness, and bile-stained vomiting typically follow. As the condition progresses, blood-tinged stool resembling jelly may be passed.

A barium enema x-ray can confirm the diagnosis—in fact, the procedure itself often cures the problem. The barium, which is dripped into the rectum under the pressure of gravity, can push the folded bowel back into its normal position. If the barium enema does not alleviate the intussusception, surgery becomes necessary. As you might expect, pediatricians are eager to evaluate a child with possible intussusception early and would much rather see some children unnecessarily than miss the diagnosis.

Some less serious, and more common, causes of abdominal pain should be noted. Gas, which causes pain by distending the intestines, can be a problem at any age, but it is especially vexing when it occurs in infants between six and sixteen weeks of age. It has a special name: *colic*. Colic makes infants cry, draw up their legs, and look miserable, sometimes for hours. The pain often recurs in a predictable fashion, every day or evening, often at the same time. Sometimes a food intolerance, tension, or nursing style that results in swallowing air can lead to colic, but more often no specific cause can be identified. It is important to remember that no matter how awful a baby with colic looks and sounds, his uncomfortable condition will not harm him. Colic eventually disappears, although it may take some time, and while it persists, parents are faced with trying a variety of measures to soothe and comfort the baby. Some examples are rocking, a ride in a car, distracting noise such as a vacuum cleaner, gentle warmth applied to the abdomen, giving fennel or chamomile tea, and careful insertion of a well lubricated cotton swab or thermometer in the rectum to stimulate the release of gas.

In older children, the most common cause of abdominal pain is a minor intestinal infection caused by a virus. The medical term for this abdominal pain, which usually is accompanied by vomiting and diarrhea, is gastroenteritis. No specific medication is effective in the treatment of viral gastroenteritis. The sick child should be given bland foods only if hungry. Warmth applied to the abdomen may ease some of the discomfort. If diarrhea lasts more than ten days or if it contains blood or large amounts of mucus the child's stool is often tested for bacteria or parasites. Meanwhile, treat the vomiting and diarrhea as described in those chapters and watch for signs of dehydration: dry, puckered skin, lips, and eyes; sunken fontanel (the soft spot on top of the infant's skull); or no urine production for six to eight hours. Dehydration can cause serious problems, so it is very important for a child with an intestinal infection to drink as much fluid as possible. If he is vomiting, allow him to rest before offering fluids, however. (See chapter on vomiting.)

Bacterial intestinal infections are less common than those caused by viruses. Food poisoning, the result of eating spoiled food, usually causes pain and sudden, recurrent vomiting. The symptoms may begin a half hour to eight hours after eating contaminated food and typically last three to five hours. Most children feel well soon after, although sometimes diarrhea will follow. Fever may also occur but is relatively unusual.

Other types of bacterial infections of the intestinal tract cause fever, vomiting, cramps, and diarrhea which may persist for several days. Stools often contain blood and mucus and may be very frequent. A sample of the stool should be cultured and if a bacteria is isolated, the child may be treated with antibiotics. In some situations, notably if salmonella bacteria are recovered, antibiotics actually prolong the length of time the germ is carried and do little to shorten the illness. In any case, you should comfort the child and make sure he gets lots of liquids, since these remedies are effective no matter what the source of the gastroenteritis.

Very severe symptoms or the passage of any large amount of blood always warrant a visit to the doctor. But small amounts of bloody spotting or streaking may also be caused by tears in the rectum from rapid passage of stools, straining, or large bowel movements, and these are not cause for alarm. External irritations may be soothed by ointments such as A & D or zinc oxide.

Abdominal pain can also originate in organs other than the intestines. Hepatitis, an inflammation of the liver that is caused by many viruses, sometimes produces tenderness and aching below the ribs on the right side of the abdomen. Another sign of hepatitis is jaundice, a yellow discoloration of the skin and the white of the eye—although many children with hepatitis do not develop jaundice. Other signs that point to hepatitis are dark urine and light, whitish stools. There is no specific treatment for hepatitis—you just have to wait for the liver to recover, but any of the symptoms mentioned above should be reported to your doctor anyway.

A twisted ovary or ruptured ovarian cyst may cause excruciating pain in the lower abdomen to the side of the navel in even very young girls. The pain is sharp and may be intermittent or persistent. Consult your doctor, who may call for tests to pinpoint the problem. Pain in the same area could be caused by infection of the uterus or Fallopian tubes, in which case there will often be fever and a vaginal discharge. The doctor may take a cervical culture and prescribe appropriate antibiotics.

In boys of any age, pain in the lower abdomen, groin, or scrotum, together with any blue-purple discoloration of the scrotum, suggest a twisting of the testicle, a medical emergency! The pain that accompanies this problem is usually very severe, but while older children will tell you what hurts, babies cannot. Call your doctor if you suspect this is the cause of your son's pain.

Remember that abdominal pain can also be caused by illnesses located outside the abdomen, such as a sore throat, an ear infection, pneumonia, or a urinary-tract infection. Usually, an accompanying symptom will point you in the right direction. For example, a urinary-tract infection may be accompanied by back pain or the urge to urinate more frequently than usual, and a young child may suddenly have daytime "accidents." Drooling can be a clue in a child too young to complain about a sore throat. Rapid breathing could indicate pneumonia.

What about chronic abdominal pain? We are often asked if a child can get ulcers. In today's hurried and harried world, it sometimes seems that children are entitled to ulcers, and they do occur—but very occasionally. Children may also very rarely suffer from colitis, a chronic irritation of the intestine characterized by recurring lower abdominal pain, diarrhea (often containing blood), anemia, weight loss, fever, and fatigue.

Many children express tension through what parents call a "sensitive stomach." The little girl who has abdominal pains shortly after the birth of a sibling, the youngster who awakens each weekday morning with a belly ache, and the older child who feels butterflies in his stomach before a school test are all reacting to tension. If a child chronically complains of a belly ache, the symptom should not be ignored. The cause of his pain may be emotional, but it could also be constipation, food intolerance, allergy, or parasites. In any case, it is appropriate to bring abdominal pain that lasts more than a few hours or recurs to the attention of your pediatrician.

Fortunately most abdominal pain goes away, and children are soon raiding the icebox and tearing about.

Diarrhea

Diarrhea is usually a symptom of a minor illness—but it is a major annoyance! Most children have at least one episode of loose stools, and many children have diarrhea many times. As you change seemingly endless diapers and sets of soiled clothes, you may find yourself wishing there was a magic cure.

Runny stools may be caused by an intestinal infection, dietary excesses, food intolerance or allergy, medications that alter the intestines' normal bacterial balance, or intestinal irritation. Emotional stress can also produce diarrhea. Some relatively rare disorders, such as colitis—chronic inflammation of the bowel—may also cause diarrhea, but are usually accompanied by signs of illness such as growth failure or weight loss. Even teething is often associated with loose stools, although we don't know why this is so.

The first question to ask is, "Is it really diarrhea?"

In infancy, stools tend to be loose and watery all the time. Look for big water rings on the diaper around the stool and a doubling of the baby's normal number of stools. If these indications are *not* present, you may be dealing with the passing effect of a chili pepper in mother's diet, not the symptom of an illness.

In older children diagnosis is more straightforward. The appearance of the stool itself tells how fast fecal matter is moving through the intestines (the transit time). If it is moving a little faster than normal, the color may be yellow. If it is moving a lot faster, the color is green because the stool has not had time to turn brown! If the stool is black and the consistency of tar, it may contain blood from the upper area of the small intestine. A stool that contains red blood may indicate bleeding further down toward the rectum. Blood can signify a bacterial intestinal infection, polyps, colitis, irritation caused by frequent bowel movements or, most commonly, a small tear in the rectum or anus from a forceful bowel movement. Hemorrhoids, incidently, are exceedingly rare in children. Diarrhea not brought on by stomach upsets or food allergies is usually caused by one of a number of viruses—

rotavirus, Coxsackie, echovirus, or one of many other organisms. There is no specific treatment for illnesses caused by viruses, but they generally run their course in five to seven days. Diarrhea may persist longer, however. Sometimes, because the intestinal lining is inflamed and irritated, diarrhea continues for ten to fourteen days, and during that period some foods are poorly digested.

Anyone who has dealt with two weeks of diarrhea will immediately ask what can be done to stop it. Over-the-counter preparations claiming to check diarrhea are not very effective. Prescription medication, while effective for older children, may be risky and may have unpleasant side effects. Unless we have a strong suspicion that the cause of diarrhea is a bacterial or parasitic organism, our initial approach involves changes in diet, extra fluids (necessary to maintain proper mineral balance and to avoid dehydration), and lots of patience. Recommended fluids include breast milk, flat sodas, diluted broth, diluted flavored rice water, and electrolyte solutions (Pedialyte, Infalyte). Solids may be given if the child wants them and is not vomiting. Be sure to choose foods known to slow down bowel motility: Bananas; Rice, rice cereal, rice crackers; grated Apples, applesauce; white-bread Toast. Remember it as the BRAT diet! Neutral foods such as chicken, eggs, and carrots may also be given. Stimulating foods such as bran, prunes, citrus fruits, and spinach are best avoided, and soy-based products are often substituted for cow's milk and its products during the first two to three days of a diarrhea attack. The diet may be liberalized after a few days because dietary imbalances may in themselves prolong diarrhea.

If the condition fails to resolve as expected, a bacterial or parasitic infection may be the cause. Diarrhea that begins suddenly, is accompanied by high fever and lethargy, and is characterized by very frequent, sometimes bloody and foul-smelling stools is particularly likely to be caused by bacterial organisms. Any of these symptoms should be reported to your doctor without delay. If your child has recently returned from a camping trip and develops diarrhea, *Giardia* (a common parasite) must be suspected.

In either of these cases, your doctor may decide to send samples of the stool to a laboratory for microscopic examination and culture. (Occasionally, an organism that can be treated is found, but most of the time the cultures are negative. Then all we can do is wait a little longer and provide supportive care.) Some types of bacterial gastroenteritis require vigorous treatment, and some must be reported to state health departments as well so that day-care centers can be informed.

If the child is becoming dehydrated, it will be necessary to compensate for fluid loss by having him drink more. The signs of dehydration include dry, wrinkled skin, a sunken fontanel (the soft spot on top of the infant's skull), crying without tear production, dry mouth and lips, and more than six to eight hours between urination. Dehydration is more likely in infants than in older children. It tends to occur in those who cannot drink extra fluid, either because of concurrent vomiting, abdominal pain, and mouth sores, or because they are just too weak. If dehydration becomes serious, children can be given extra fluid intravenously. Sometimes—but not always—this entails admission to the hospital.

Some children get chronic diarrhea, sometimes lasting for months. The most common kind occurs in toddlers and is known as *nonspecific diarrhea of childhood*. Usually it is impossible to identify the cause of the diarrhea. Stools may range from fairly solid to entirely liquid, running down the child's legs. The hallmark of this condition is that the child retains his energy, gains weight, and has normal stool cultures. Although some manipulations of diet may be tried, there is generally no treatment for this form of diarrhea. The toddlers affected just travel with extra diapers and extra clothes. Very often, by the time the doctor has shared the parents' frustration in trying to eliminate potentially aggravating foods from the child's diet, the loose stools mysteriously subside.

Less benign, though, is *significant chronic diarrhea*, which typically leads to weight loss and subseqently to growth failure. Therefore, testing for conditions such as colitis and malabsorption is often considered if a child fails to gain weight. In the presence of significant chronic diarrhea, malabsorption of nutrients is often a problem. Stools tend to be foul-smelling and frothy as well as loose. Malabsorption occurs when intestinal function is so swift that food cannot be processed sufficiently for the body to absorb necessary nutrients from it. Among the causes of malabsorption are food intolerances, allergies, parasitic diseases, and such chronic conditions as cystic fibrosis and celiac disease. Tests can be performed on the stool as well as on the blood to detect these (rare) conditions.

Fortunately, patience, fortitude, and loving care for the child with diarrhea are usually all parents need to provide. A hint you may find helpful for treatment of little buttocks irritated from a bad episode of loose stools: apply a paste made of cornstarch mixed with milk of magnesia. This concoction neutralizes the acid in stools that burn the skin. It often works when the usual salves for diaper rash fail.

The bottom line on childhood diarrhea: most of the time you simply wait it out. It is not fun but also not too serious. That's easy for you to say, Doctor!

Constipation

Does my child need to have a daily bowel movement? What does a normal stool look like? How can I tell if my child is constipated? When is constipation a problem? These are all question parents often ask us.

Children do not need to have a daily bowel movement. Passing stools as often as two to four times a day or as seldom as once every six days can be normal as long as the stool is soft, the pattern is consistent, and there is no pain, blood, or loose stool. Well-meaning parents may give a child strong bowel stimulants only to discover that they have replaced relatively innocuous constipation with cramps and diarrhea. We advise our parents to look at their child—not at their calendar!

It is perfectly normal for babies to grunt and groan, turn red, and squirm during bowel movements. They are not considered constipated unless they go more than five to seven days without a bowel movement and their stools become hard and dry.

A child who actually is constipated may have painful bowel movements or be unable to complete a movement even though the urge to evacuate is strong. The stools may be very dry, hard and pelletlike, bulky, or contain blood. Soiling (usually with brownish liquid) between bowel movements may also occur.

Only rarely is constipation cause for serious alarm. There are only two or three really serious causes of constipation in children that you need to look for.

Hirschsprung's disease, a very rare congenital malformation, causes chronic constipation in infants. In this condition, the nerve endings in the colon or rectum have not developed and the rectum does not sense the need for a bowel movement. Constipation in children with Hirschsprung's disease begins soon after birth and fails to respond to the usual simple treatments outlined below. The problem is corrected by surgically removing the segment of bowel that lacks nerve endings.

Second, constipation in a baby less than about fifteen months old, accompanied by progressive muscle weakness, especially in the face (inability to smile or suck successfully, excess drooling), suggests infant botulism and should be evaluated by a doctor at once. This illness, which results in nerve paralysis, is caused by a toxin released by the bacterium *Clostridium botulinum.* This toxin has been recovered from honey, molasses, and corn syrup in various parts of the United States; it is therefore vital to check with your doctor before giving any of these foods to a baby under the age of fifteen months.

A third, very rare, cause for concern is intestinal obstruction. In that case green bile-stained vomiting will accompany constipation and should be brought to the doctor's attention fast. But again, this condition is very rare.

Most of the time, constipation clears up by itself. Changes in diet are usually all that is necessary to relieve it. Infants who are breast- or formula-fed may need more fluid or an adjustment of formula. Nursing mothers sometimes find that additional fruits, roughage, and fluids in their own diet produce the desired effect in their infants. Formulas with soy or with high iron content are apt to cause hard, dark stools in some babies; you may need to experiment with different kinds of formulas. If dietary changes are not effective, dilute prune juice (1 ounce of juice to 2 ounces of water) or sugar water (1 teaspoon of granulated sugar to 4 ounces of water) may do the trick. For older children, diluted cherry or grape juice as well as prunes and bulk-forming cereals such as bran may alleviate constipation. Foods such as bananas, rice, apples, and dairy products should be avoided as long as a child is troubled by constipation.

If diet change does not work, consult your pediatrician. Laxatives and enemas should never be used before discussing the matter with your doctor. If your child's doctor decides you need to stimulate the rectum, use a rectal thermometer or cotton swab lubricated with petroleum jelly or a pediatric glycerin suppository. Half a suppository is adequate for infants, a whole one for children over two years old. Hold the buttocks together for two or three minutes after insertion for best results.

Problems with constipation often arise during toilet training. This process involves learning to control the rectal muscles, and a child may use his newly acquired ability to hold back his stools for a variety of reasons: power struggles with parents, manipulation, fear of losing control, fear of growing up and being independent, fear of making a mess, or simply fear that the bowel movement may hurt. Toilet training should be relaxed if a child is having trouble with constipation. For example, a toddler might be offered the option of a diaper for stools, or toilet training might be suspended entirely for a while. If you're making a great many grown-up demands on your child all at once, ease up on some of them until he gets healthy elimination down pat.

Older children may also hold back their stool as a consequence of anger, frustration, feelings of powerlessness, or the need to control something, anything. If the habit becomes entrenched, a child may require long-term counseling and support by his doctor. Stool-holding can lead to painful bowel movements, tears in the rectum, and spotty bleeding. Dietary changes will help soften stools and warm baths and soothing ointments, such as those used for diaper rash, can be used to treat anal tears.

Most often, however, constipation in older children from "holding it in" happens because time is short or because another activity seems more important at the time or even because the available bathroom is unappealing. Besides making sure their children get plenty of fluids and roughage, parents should also make sure kids have enough time to go to the bathroom. For an older child, it may be helpful to establish a scheduled time for going to the bathroom. He might try going the same time each day and remaining for a few minutes. Parents can also reassure their child that constipation is temporary and that he will soon be back to normal.

Common Childhood Ailments

*C*hildren can be affected by most of the ills that beset adults and a few more besides. Every normal, healthy child is sure to have some infections (including the now fortunately rare "childhood diseases"), skin problems, or disorders of one or another body system. Most children come through these troubles without complications or permanent aftereffects. Still, parents worry when their child is not bouncing with health. Knowing the nature of the ailments your child may encounter and what to do about them gives you a head start on dealing with this inevitable part of growing up.

Infections

How often do children get infections? Which infections should we worry about? How do we recognize serious illnesses and how do we nurse and comfort our children through those that are less serious but equally exhausting?

It is difficult to estimate the number and type of infections the average healthy child will get. It often depends on the child's age and his exposure to other children. The immune system of a very young infant is not as sophisticated as that of an older child, and therefore the same organism may cause a more serious illness in a baby than in an older sibling. Since children share germs when they play together, some pediatricians feel that an infant's increased susceptibility to serious illness overrides any benefit of being with large groups of children. Others feel it is important for babies to socialize with large groups of infants early in life despite the increased risk of illness. The inescapable truth is that healthy children do get colds and other infections no matter what course parents follow. We can only do our best to prepare for them, understand them, and take appropriate precautions to reduce their frequency when possible. Preventive measures include making sure children get the appropriate vaccinations, recognizing when they need more rest or a better diet, taking care not to expose them to anyone known to be ill, and teaching them the importance of cleanliness (good handwashing technique, for example—important for children *and* parents). (See chapters on immunization and good health habits.)

There are differences as well as similarities among viral, bacterial, and parasitic infections. Although an initial symptom such as a sore throat might be common to both a bacterial (strep) and a viral (Coxsackie) illness, the course, consequences, and treatment are entirely different. A strep infection, confirmed by a throat culture, requires treatment with antibiotics. A viral sore throat responds only to the "tincture of time." Both illnesses may be accompanied by rashes, and both can cause abdominal pain. However, only strep throat can, though rarely, lead to the complication of rheumatic fever. In order to anticipate and prevent certain complications, it helps to know what infection one is dealing with.

General symptoms such as fever, fatigue, loss of appetite, and enlargement of the lymph nodes are common to many infectious diseases. When there is an infection in the body, even a very mild one, the lymph nodes closest to the infection will become enlarged, reflecting the body's attempt to fight the infection. The lymph nodes most commonly involved are those in the neck, behind the ears, under the arms, and in the groin. They may be felt as small, round, movable bumps just under the skin that are often tender. They can remain enlarged for several weeks or even months, long after the symptoms of the infection have subsided. Often the nodes will again become enlarged the next time a child has a cold or other infection.

All infectious diseases share certain characteristics. First, they are caused by a germ, usually coming from outside the child's body. Second, they always have an incubation period, a prodromal period, and a contagious period. The incubation period begins when the child comes in contact with the disease and lasts until the child first shows signs of illness. During this time, which can be anywhere from hours to months, the child feels fine, but the germ is multiplying and settling into tissues. Incubation is followed by the prodromal period, during which the child has vague, nonspecific symptoms such as fatigue or grouchiness. The contagious period, during which the child can make other people sick, begins at the end of the incubation period, technically includes the prodromal period, and varies in length depending on the illness.

How do children pick up germs? Usually from other kids! Germs can be transmitted through saliva when children share bottles or toys; they can be transmitted through droplets of mucus from the nose when children cough and sneeze near one another; they can be transmitted through fecal matter when a caretaker changes an infant's diaper and does not wash her hands thoroughly before preparing food, or when a child touches a dirty changing table and then sucks on his contaminated fingers. One can become paranoid about the great variety of possible exposures, but an awareness of the way germs are spread can also help parents protect their child from unnecessary exposure.

Parents often ask if one child can catch an ear infection from another. The answer is, well, sort of. The germ that causes an infection may come courtesy of another child, but it does not go directly from the ear of one child to the ear of the other. (It can also come as a complication of, say, a cold.) Whether the germ causes an infection in the ear of the second child, or in the throat, lungs, or elsewhere, depends on luck, the child's immune system and anatomy, and perhaps other susceptibility factors as well.

We are also often asked whether splashing in puddles and wading in wet boots, playing outside in cold weather, or running about without a sweater or hat will cause illness. Despite the fact that we have all grown up hearing they do, there is no actual evidence to support these contentions.

The period of contagion—when one child can infect another—usually begins about twenty-four hours before the child seems ill (and at that point no one knows the child is getting sick!). How long it lasts depends on the type of illness. The sick child may remain contagious for two to three days after the first signs of illness appear and for twenty-four to forty-eight hours after a fever has disappeared. When is it safe for a child who has been ill to return to school? Parents should consider the following points. First, it is important to protect other children from a contagious child. Second, it is essential to protect the child who has been ill from getting worn out and possibly suffering a relapse. The only way to be sure is to keep the child at home a day or two after he seems completely recovered. This advice is frequently difficult to follow when there are pressures on parents to return to work, when there are other sick kids at home, or when the child is eager to be out and about.

How safe is it for a pregnant woman to be exposed to a child with an infectious disease? It is probably a sound policy to keep a sick child away from a pregnant woman if possible. How dangerous an infection may be depends on the nature of the disease, the stage of the pregnancy, and the pregnant woman's previous health experience. Since various illnesses, such as herpes and rubella, may affect the fetus in different ways, it is important that a pregnant woman check with her doctor if she has been exposed to an infectious disease. Although most illnesses do not affect the fetus, being sick *and* pregnant doesn't make you feel great.

Adults in general may have more serious reactions to "childhood diseases" than their children do. For instance, adults with chicken pox tend to have more spots and run higher fevers, and adults with measles develop serious complications, such as encephalitis, much more often than children. Blood tests can let you know if you are immune to various illnesses. If you are not, exercise extreme caution, or, with a doctor's advice, start the necessary immunizations.

Regardless of whether the illness is viral, bacterial, or parasitic, parents want to know how to treat their sick child. Should my child stay in bed? Should my child have extra naps? Can my child play outside? Can my child ride in the car pool or go to the park? Should I keep my child especially warm? What should I feed my child? Can my child have visitors?

There are no uniform answers to these questions. Most children will pace themselves fairly well when they are sick. They will want to sleep and rest more than they do normally. As they feel better, they will become more active. Some children seek the comfort of their beds and others prefer to collapse on a couch or in their parents' room. Some children like to stay in their pajamas, while others like to dress and follow familiar routines. For a very fussy, exhausted youngster, parents can arrange quiet activities that make it easy for him to doze off to sleep when he feels like it. If the weather is warm and a child prefers to sit or play outside, being in the fresh air is certainly at least as healthy as being inside. As for taking the sick child to the park or riding in a car pool, a parent must evaluate the chances of the sick child infecting other children. This rule also applies to inviting friends over or accepting invitations to parties. Many close friendships have been strained by the thoughtless exposure of a sick child to healthy playmates.

There is no need to dress the sick child any warmer than usual. In fact, if a child has a fever, it is best to keep him lightly dressed so the temperature can come down and the child can be as comfortable as possible.

To feed or not to feed? Most children lose their appetite when they are ill. Their reaction to eating or drinking often depends on the particular symptoms they are experiencing. A child with a sore throat will not want to eat and will prefer to drink cool fluids. A child with abdominal pain or a child who is vomiting may appropriately refuse any food or drink. If a child is at risk of dehydration, however, parents should encourage sips of fluid, even if the child is not thirsty.

In the following section we describe some of the most common viral, bacterial, and parasitic infections seen in children. We hope these discussions will help you recognize the symptoms of various illnesses and give you an idea of the course they will take and the kinds of treatment that are appropriate.

Viral Infections

Many viral infections have unique symptoms that make them easy to identify. Other viral infections are more difficult to diagnose since different viruses may cause similar symptoms. There is no specific treatment for most simple viral infections. Some new antiviral agents are reserved for very severe illnesses or special circumstances. Antibiotics have no effect on viruses. The best we can do is to provide comfort and try to reduce a fever, soothe a cough, stop a runny nose, or supply appropriate liquids to a dehydrated child. Viral infections can linger, and occasionally a child may develop a secondary bacterial infection. Some viral infections can cause serious problems, but happily, most run their course without any complications.

Colds

Colds make everybody miserable, but there isn't much that anyone can do to prevent or treat them. We know that colds are caused by a number of different respiratory viruses. Children seem to get the greatest number of colds between the ages of two and five—sometimes as many as eight or more a year. In fact, it often seems easier to count the days your child *hasn't* had a runny nose rather than the other way around.

Since cold viruses are spread from person to person by close contact, crowded areas such as day-care centers are natural breeding grounds for recurrent colds. Bottles, pacifiers, and toys moist with saliva are commonly passed back and forth among children. We used to think that sneezing was the primary means of transmitting cold viruses, but it turns out now that hand-to-hand contact may be just as important.

Most of us are all too familiar with the annoying symptoms of a cold, which typically last about seven to ten days. After exposure, there is an incubation period of three to four days during which the virus becomes established. The clear, drippy nasal discharge and hacking cough are the result of excess mucus produced when the inner lining of the nose is inflamed. The mucus runs back down the throat, especially when the child is lying down, so the cough may well be worse at night. The eyes may be red and watery, and small amounts of discharge may form a crust along the eyelids, most visible after a night's sleep. During the following three to four days the cough may persist, and the nasal mucus may turn thick and yellow or green. As the child recovers, intermittent coughing may persist for up to a month. Children with colds are usually contagious one or two days before the onset of symptoms and for three or four days thereafter.

Does getting chilled cause a cold? There is no evidence that wind or cold weather influence susceptibility, and no known product or life-style has been shown to prevent colds. In fact, about all one can do is to avoid close contact with anyone who has a cold. Changes in diet, vitamins, or activity seem to have no impact on the number or duration of colds.

Nor is there any specific treatment for a cold. Antibiotics are ineffective because they do not work against viruses. They are useful only for treating some of the bacterial complications of colds, such as ear or sinus infections. Extra rest may be of some benefit, but strict bed rest and constant bundling are not necessary. Neither is chicken soup, but at least it tastes good!

Pediatric-strength medications to relieve stuffiness (such as over-the-counter decongestants or decongestant-antihistamines) may be helpful, but they have some undesirable side effects, such as irritability, drowsiness, headache, and increased heart rate and blood pressure. The younger the child, the greater the likelihood that the side effects will exceed the benefits. We feel these medications are generally unsafe for infants who weigh less than fifteen to eighteen pounds. Doses for children under two years old are usually not specified, even though many of these medications are safe for younger children. Ask your doctor in advance to tell you the medicine he prefers and the dose for your child.

If daytime symptoms are not too severe, consider giving medication at bedtime only. Medicinal nose drops should not be used unless prescribed by your doctor for specific, limited situations.

Here are some things that may make your child feel more comfortable. Nasal congestion may be eased by elevating the head of the bed (a rolled up blanket under the mattress works well), or by using a cool mist vaporizer or humidifier. Encourage your child to drink extra fluids in order to loosen mucus. But all in all, the best treatment for a cold —at any age—is sympathy and patience.

Just as there isn't much you can do to prevent or cure the cold itself, there is not much protection against complications; some children are just more prone to them than others. Some signs of complications that may require an office visit are:

❑ A rectal temperature greater than 101 degrees or unexpectedly ill appearance in an infant less than three months old could signify a bacterial infection on top of a cold. Most pediatricians feel it best to examine such a baby, and many will perform a blood test if bacterial infection is suspected. The younger the child, the greater the likelihood of a serious infection. (See chapter on fever.)

❑ The onset of fever at what ought to be the end of a cold may be due to an ear infection. If this happens, the cough may worsen or deepen, eye drainage might begin or resume, and the child may awaken at night because of ear pain. Tugging at the ears, unexplained crying, and vomiting are other common signs of ear infection.

❑ Rapid, shallow breathing, especially at a rate greater than sixty times per minute, could indicate a lung infection such as bronchitis or pneumonia. Most children with a lower respiratory tract infection will have a deep cough that keeps them up at night and a diminished ability to eat due to rapid, labored breathing. In interpreting a rapid respiratory rate, please remember that blocked nostrils or fever can themselves raise the rate of breathing even if there are no lung problems. Lung problems are generally signaled by additional symptoms: flaring of the nostrils, spreading of the ribs with breathing, or other indications that respiration is impaired or requires additional effort. Chest pain, especially when the child inhales, suggests a possible problem in the lungs. A child with this symptom should be examined.

❑ A combination of thick, green nasal discharge, cough, fever, and bad breath could indicate a sinus infection. Older children may develop characteristic sinus pain behind the eyes and forehead, but children under the age of nine typically do not. (The sinus cavities are formed at different ages, so some are not even present in toddlers and infants.) X-rays and ultrasound examination can be used to diagnose sinusitis in children over the age of two with varying degrees of accuracy. Most doctors are reluctant to obtain x-rays each time a diagnosis is sought, so children are sometimes treated on the basis of clinical suspicion alone.

☐ Swelling or bright red or purple discoloration of the skin over an eyelid or cheek could indicate a very serious bacterial infection. Infection around the eye (periorbital cellulitis) requires prompt attention because it can lead to serious infection of the globe of the eye (orbital cellulitis). Both of these complications, as well as buccal cellulitis (of the cheek), are associated with bacterial infection of the blood. These conditions need to be treated by your child's doctor promptly and vigorously, often with intravenous antibiotics.

☐ Pinkeye, or conjunctivitis, is a redness of the white portion of the eye, usually accompanied by the drainage of pus. It may be confused with periorbital cellulitis because of the swelling and discoloration of the eyelid. But conjunctivitis is usually confined to the white of the eye, whereas periorbital cellulitis involves a wider area, the eyelid. If it fails to clear up by itself after three days, or if there is fever or copious discharge, call your doctor. Conjunctivitis is highly contagious; affected children should not have contact with others, especially newborns, until it has completely resolved.

☐ Sore—and very red—throat or tonsils, even in the presence of a cold, could signify strep throat. The typical sore throat that precedes a cold goes away in a day or two. A child with lingering throat pain should probably be examined, and a throat culture may be indicated.

Occasionally, then, the simple cold is not so simple. But most of the time children sail through colds and are best helped by being reassured that it will go away. After the initial infectious period has passed, children should resume normal activities and return to school. Confinement and bed rest do not seem to shorten a cold and may even add to the child's misery. There is an old saying that if you do not treat a cold it lasts a week; if you treat it the cold lasts seven days. Wonders of modern medicine notwithstanding, this pretty much sums up the situation with colds at the present time.

Flu (INFLUENZA)

We often speak casually of "the flu" when describing any viral illness accompanied by fever and achiness, but this one is "The Flu." A number of influenza viruses exist (called types A, B, and C), but all forms of this highly epidemic illness, which usually strikes in winter, are characterized by fever, shaking chills, aching muscles, headache, and a hacking cough. A sore throat, watery eyes, and a runny nose may add to the child's discomfort. Flu appears suddenly but the symptoms may last two to three weeks. Most kids with flu feel terrible and are not opposed to resting. They have little appetite, and since a sore throat is a common symptom, they tend to prefer fluids to solid food.

The flu virus is spread from person to person by direct contact with saliva, with particles released into the air by coughing, or with mucus-contaminated articles like toys or bottles. The incubation period is short, usually one to three days. When there is flu in the community, it is usually no secret, for this is a highly contagious illness. A person is most contagious during the twenty-four hours preceding the illness—before he knows he is coming down with something —and continuing up to a week thereafter. Flu is frequently spread from school-age children to adults and younger children, and often some family members are still recovering just as others are beginning to feel the first symptoms.

As with so many other viral infections, treatment consists primarily of comforting the patient and giving acetaminophen to relieve a high fever or achiness. Some doctors prefer not to give aspirin to children and teenagers with influenza because of its possible association with Reye's syndrome. (See section on chicken pox.) The antiviral drug amantidine, commonly given to adults to reduce the severity of the symptoms of influenza A, is occasionally prescribed for children who are severely ill or who have other serious chronic conditions such as cystic fibrosis or sickle cell anemia.

We are often asked about preventive immunization against influenza. Vaccines are available for some strains of flu virus and clearly are appropriate for those children with serious chronic diseases. But despite the fact that some authorities have advocated routine flu shots for all children, most pediatricians are reluctant to administer an annual injection for an illness that is generally mild in healthy children.

Enteroviruses (COXSACKIE, ECHOVIRUS)

Although most parents are not familiar with the enteroviruses, there are many, and they are very commonly encountered, especially during the spring and summer. Typical symptoms include fever, sore throat, abdominal pain, vomiting, diarrhea, and a fine red rash that starts on the back and chest and often spreads to the face, arms, and legs. This rash usually does not itch. The symptoms can follow one another virtually in any order, making the diagnosis a little tricky at times.

An infant who is cranky, has a low-grade fever, mild diarrhea, and drooling due to a sore throat may have an enterovirus. One special variation is the so-called hand, foot, and mouth disease (Coxsackie A16) in which blisters form on the palms, soles, and inside the child's mouth. This common virus is frequently shared with older family members and is jokingly called "hoof-and-mouth disease."

The enteroviruses are spread from person to person through saliva and feces. Children who share bottles or straws or drool on one another may thus be sharing this common virus as well. Since these viruses can reside in a sick child's intestines, they may be transmitted from one child to another if parents or caretakers are not careful to wash their hands before and after changing diapers. The incubation period for most enteroviruses is three to six days. The illness usually lasts from four to six days, and the child will be contagious for up to seven days after the symptoms appear.

There is no specific treatment for enteroviruses other than for the individual symptoms. Fever and achiness may be relieved by appropriate doses of acetaminophen. Cool drinks, Popsicles, and soft, cool foods will be soothing to a sore throat. It is best to follow the child's lead in determining whether he is ready to eat solid foods. The red rash disappears spontaneously. The sores in the mouth are often the most distressing aspect of the Coxsackie virus infection. Cool liquids and acetaminophen may be helpful, but once again only time provides the cure.

Rotavirus

This virus, though little known to parents, is the most common cause of diarrhea in children between six and twenty-four months of age. It occurs throughout the world and can also affect older children and adults.

The diarrhea is usually preceded by a slight fever and some vomiting. The child may also have a cough and runny nose. Parents and caretakers are very relieved to see this illness subside, for at its peak the child may have two to ten watery, foul-smelling stools a day—for days on end. The virus is transmitted in the stool and the incubation period is five to seven days. The illness usually lasts from two to five days, but the diarrhea may persist for two to three weeks. The child is contagious for about one week after the initial onset of symptoms. Parents and caretakers must be careful to wash their hands very thoroughly after changing diapers and before preparing food.

The presence of rotavirus can now be confirmed by a simple, though expensive, stool test. Reinfection is known to occur, and often an infected older sibling or adult with no symptoms may be contagious.

There is no specifc way to eradicate this virus, and unless the child is becoming dehydrated, can be treated at home. Acetaminophen may be given in the proper dose for fever. When a child is vomiting, only sips of fluid should be given, as discussed in the chapter on vomiting. The diarrhea will eventually clear up by itself; *there is no benefit in using various antidiarrheal preparations from the pharmacy.* In fact, these will often cause the child to have cramps and feel even more uncomfortable. It is best to avoid milk and milk products during this illness and for three or four days after it has subsided, since a temporary inability to digest milk sugar (lactose) may prolong the diarrhea. A bland diet of bananas, rice, apples, and toast (the BRAT diet) is helpful during the initial course of the diarrhea.

Chicken Pox (VARICELLA)

Chicken pox is one of the most common and most contagious of childhood diseases. Children of all ages can contract chicken pox—even breast-fed infants. Despite the fact that it is highly contagious, many children are exposed to chicken pox several times before they actually come down with it. Parents frequently ask whether they should purposely have their well child play with a friend who has chicken pox so that their child will "get it over with." We do not recommend this practice. While chicken pox is most often an annoying but benign illness, there can be severe complications. It is also possible (though very unusual) to get chicken pox more than once. This is most likely to happen if the child first had the infection before he was six months old.

Chicken pox is not always easy to recognize at first. The affected child may have a mild fever and seem a bit cranky. Within twenty-four hours a rash appears which initially resembles, and may be confused with, insect bites. Typically this itchy rash begins on the chest and back. Within the next twenty-four hours these red bumps multiply and become fluid-filled blisters and subsequently crust over and form a scab. As the first pox fill and crust over, new crops may appear in other places, including the scalp, ears, eyelids, face, throat, arms and legs, penis, and vagina. Chicken pox in the eye itself may require special treatment, so your doctor should be notified if your child's eye turns red or pox are visible on the eye itself. Pox in the mouth or the throat can make swallowing painful and thus affect the child's appetite. New crops may continue to appear for four to six days. Some children feel quite well during this period, but others are miserable with a high fever, nausea, a cough, and very itchy skin.

Chicken pox is spread by contact with infected nasal or

throat secretions, and by transmission of the virus through the air, so direct contact is not necessary to catch the disease. The incubation period for chicken pox is ten to twenty-one days. The child is not contagious during this time. He is, however, contagious during the prodromal period, the twenty-four to forty-eight hours during which he is starting to feel ill but does not yet have the characteristic signs of chicken pox. The illness usually lasts for seven to ten days, from the initial fever to the final scabbing, and the child remains contagious until all the pox are scabbed over. It may then take another five to twenty days for the scabs to dry and disappear, but the child is not contagious during this time and can return to school. Parents are often concerned about whether or not the chicken pox will leave scars. It is difficult to predict which pox will scar and which will not. Deep pox on the face, especially those that have been scratched, may become small, slightly indented marks. These marks are initially dark on light skin and light on dark skin, and they fade considerably with time.

Adults who have never had chicken pox should avoid contact with children who have active chicken pox, since they can get a relatively severe case of it. Similarly, the fetus is susceptible and may have very severe complications of chicken pox, but it can only acquire the disease from its mother. There is no risk, therefore, if a pregnant woman who has already had chicken pox comes in contact with someone who has it. A newborn whose mother is susceptible is also susceptible and may have a severe case if the disease is acquired in the first five to seven days of life. After that, babies usually have cases as mild as older childrens'. Newborns whose mothers have already had chicken pox may be protected by maternal antibodies. They usually do not acquire the illness when exposed or develop a very mild case.

A child with contagious chicken pox should *not* be in

contact with adults and children with suppressed immune systems (cancer or AIDS patients, people on steroids or chemotherapy), even if they have had the disease. Such individuals are prone to develop shingles, which is a reactivation of the dormant chicken-pox virus.

A chicken-pox vaccine is currently under development, but until it is released and accepted for general use little can be done to prevent a child from getting the disease. There are, however, a number of ways to make him more comfortable when he does become ill. Intense itching can be relieved by giving the child cool baths to which baking soda or colloidal oatmeal has been added (to the point of making the water cloudy). Calamine lotion (not Caladryl) can be applied to the skin. Antihistamines such as Benadryl or stronger prescribed medications against itching may be given by mouth if necessary. Acetaminophen may be given for fever; many doctors prefer not to use aspirin because of its possible association with Reye's syndrome. Cutting the child's fingernails short and placing adhesive bandages over particularly itchy pox will reduce the likelihood of scars.

Measles (RUBEOLA)

When parents notice a fine red rash on their sick child they invariably ask, "Does my child have measles?" Many of us remember having the measles and think of it as a harmless childhood illness, but it can be quite serious. Fortunately, we do not encounter measles very often these days since children now receive the measles-mumps-rubella vaccine (MMR) when 15 months old. With rare exceptions, it gives them immunity to this disease.

A child who does come down with measles first feels cranky and achy and has a high fever. Within twenty-four hours he has a runny nose, red, watery eyes which are sensitive to bright light, and a cough. Usually about the third day a spotty red rash appears, starting along the hairline and behind the ears. Over the next two to three days the rash spreads downward to the face, chest, back, arms, and legs. The fever tends to subside at this time. There are often more red spots on the face than anywhere else on the body. The rash disappears after about five days in the same order as it developed (the face and chest may be clear before the rash disappears from the arms and legs). Most children with measles feel pretty miserable for six to nine days. Rarely, some children suffer from complications such as pneumonia, encephalitis (an infection of the brain), irritation of the cornea, and painfully infected lymph nodes. Luckily, a child who has had the measles is unlikely to get it again.

Measles virus is spread through direct contact with saliva or nasal secretions or through mucus particles when children sneeze and breathe on one another. The incubation period is eight to twelve days from exposure to the onset of symptoms.

Measles is highly contagious. A child can infect other children for about ten days beginning a day or two before he shows any signs of the illness until the fourth or fifth day after the rash has appeared. It is best not to send the child back to school until the rash has completely faded.

Once again, there is no medical treatment for this illness. Acetaminophen helps if there is a high fever and achiness. Most children feel quite sick at first and welcome a chance to lie still. Initially, appetites are poor and children should not be forced to eat. Avoiding bright lights will certainly make them more comfortable but contrary to popular belief, light will not damage the eyes in any way.

A baby who is exposed to measles before he is fifteen months old, and therefore before the time of routine immunization, can be given immune globulin. Although it may not prevent the child from getting the disease, it may at least modify the severity of the symptoms. The child must then be immunized with the MMR vaccine later for lasting immunity.

Mumps

Once very common, mumps is now rarely seen thanks to the widespread use of the measles-mumps-rubella vaccine (MMR) which is given to children at fifteen months. Those children who do still get mumps are usually under the age of fifteen months or if older, have not been immunized for one reason or another. Mumps is usually a mild though memorable illness. Because it is the parotid salivary gland that is irritated by the mumps virus, the child has a chipmunk appearance, with swelling on one or both sides of the jaw. He typically has difficulty talking and chewing, and the swelling makes it hard to feel the rear angle of the jaw. Mumps is spread through saliva and nasal secretions. The incubation period is about twelve to twenty-five days. Most children with mumps have a fever and some generalized aches and pains two to three days before the swelling appears. The swelling itself usually lasts about a week. Children are contagious twenty-four to forty-eight hours before they have any symptoms at all and until one day after the swelling has gone —about seven to ten days in all. Can a child who has received the MMR vaccine or one who has already had mumps play with a contagious child? Yes, as long as the child has been immunized at least four to five weeks prior to contact with the contagious friend.

About ten percent of teenage boys may experience testicular inflammation or orchitis while they have mumps. Of course the first question parents ask is "Will my son become sterile?" This is a very unlikely possibility since typically only one testicle is affected and the incidence of inflammation is so low. Less than ten percent of teenage girls and women with mumps experience pain in the lower abdomen near the ovaries. The discomfort is usually felt only on one side and does not affect reproduction.

Other rare but worrisome complications of the mumps virus include meningitis and hearing loss. A child with meningitis may complain of a severe headache, be unable to move his head up and down, have a high fever, and be very drowsy and lethargic. Any child with these symptoms should be promptly examined by a doctor.

Curiously, in spite if its spectacular symptoms, mumps is not always easy to identify. There are a variety of viruses that cause swelling of the parotid gland, a mild fever, and general achiness. A blood test can be done to identify which virus is involved if the doctor is not certain.

The lymph nodes located close to the jaw can also become infected by various other viruses or bacteria and the swelling that results may be mistaken for mumps. Any time a child's neck is red, tender, and swollen, he should be examined by a doctor.

About forty percent of all children who contract mumps have such a mild case that it may go unnoticed. Many adults who do not remember having had mumps may nevertheless have been infected and are therefore immune. If it is important to determine whether or not an adult has had mumps, it is best to check the blood for the antibody. Even Mom may have trouble remembering which of her children had mumps thirty-five years ago!

As is the case with so many other viral illnesses there is no specific treatment for mumps. Children will rest if they are particularly tired. Acetaminophen may help the aches and pains as will cool compresses gingerly placed over the swelling. Cool liquids such as milkshakes initially may be the diet of choice. Avoid giving the child with mumps acidic drinks such as orange juice and ginger ale, as they stimulate the affected glands and may cause pain.

German Measles (RUBELLA)

Once very common, German measles has become a rare illness, since children are now given measles-mumps-rubella vaccine (MMR) when they are fifteen months old. When it does occur, German measles, or rubella, usually afflicts older children or teenagers who have not been immunized. Rubella is of concern because it can cause birth defects in children of unimmunized women who contract the disease early in pregnancy. The MMR immunization, on the other hand, does not transmit German measles to the fetus, and is thus safely given to women of childbearing age. Children who develop a fever and a rash as a reaction to their vaccination likewise do not have "measles" and cannot transmit this illness.

A young child with German measles does not seem very sick. The first sign of illness is usually a light pink-red rash that does not itch. It initially appears on the forehead and then quickly progresses down the body to the chest and back. Finally, by the beginning of the third day, it appears on the arms and legs. The duration and location of the rash can vary, but usually by the end of the third day the rash has disappeared completely. Typically the lymph nodes in the neck and behind the ear are enlarged and mildly tender, and the child has a slight fever and runny nose.

Older children and teenagers may experience more discomfort; their rash is often preceded by a few days of low fever, achiness, mildly red eyes, slight runny nose, sore throat, and a cough. These early symptoms disappear when the rash breaks out. Very occasionally a teenager with German measles may develop a painful swelling of the joints. Many children get such a mild case of German measles that they show no signs of illness, though they do develop the antibodies.

The virus is spread through nasal secretions and saliva, and the incubation period is fourteen to twenty-one days. A child with rubella is contagious for about ten days, beginning a day or two before the appearance of the rash, and lasting two to five days after it has disappeared. Yes, with rubella a child may be contagious even after the rash is gone!

The unfortunate infant infected by the rubella virus while in the mother's uterus may not only have extensive birth defects but also may be contagious and therefore capable of spreading the virus for as long as a year or more after birth. This is a problem for pregnant nurses working in hospital nurseries where they might be exposed to a newborn with the illness before a diagnosis is made.

There is no specific treatment for German measles. Acetaminophen may be given if a child has aches and pains or fever. Most children are quite comfortable eating, sleeping and moving about—though they get tired of being isolated from their susceptible friends. The good news is that rubella does seem to be a once-in-a-lifetime illness with full immunity conferred by the naturally acquired antibody. There is some question as to whether the vaccine provides lifetime protection. For this reason some doctors like to do a blood test to see if teenage girls show evidence of continuing immunity and, if not, to revaccinate them. Young women planning to become pregnant should certainly be tested if they have any doubt about immunity and be vaccinated or revaccinated if necessary.

Herpes (HSV)

There are two forms of the Herpes simplex virus. HSV I, which commonly infects children, typically makes its appearance as the well-known cold sore or fever blister. This virus should not be confused with its more notorious cousin HSV II, which causes genital herpes, a very uncommon problem in children.

HSV stays with us for life. Following the initial infection, the virus becomes dormant but remains capable of causing symptoms at a later time. We do not know why recurrent outbreaks are common in some children and rare in others. These outbreaks may be triggered by emotional stress, fatigue, trauma, sun exposure, or other illnesses, or they may occur spontaneously, without apparent cause.

HSV I frequently causes an infection so mild that a child does not appear to be sick at all. In other cases, its effects are more severe: the child may abruptly develop a high fever, cry inconsolably, and drool profusely because the gums and inside of the mouth are so very sore. The blisters of HSV I are filled with virus and the infection spreads by direct contact with a blister or with saliva, which also contains the virus. Thus a child with an HSV I blister can suck his thumb and cause another blister on his hand.

The incubation period for HSV I is about six days and the acute infection may last for five to ten days. A child with a herpes infection is most contagious when the blisters first appear and remains so for about a week. But the virus can be spread even when the child does not feel ill. This is a distressing circumstance for it is difficult to determine when a child with an HSV I infection can return to school or even whether, since this illness is so benign, a child with a cold sore should be kept home at all.

On rare occasions the herpes virus may cause a very serious eye infection. If there is any question about the severity of an HSV infection your child should be examined by his doctor.

HSV II is a problem seen in adults, sexually active teenagers, and newborn babies exposed to the virus during birth. The virus infects areas such as the mouth, nipples, vagina, and penis. Blisters appear either singly or in groups, and may be painless or quite painful. However, the effects of the virus on the newborn may be quite devastating, causing severe brain infection and even death. Mothers with active herpes in the genital area at the time of delivery may be advised to deliver by cesarean section.

The incubation period for HSV II has not been clearly determined but we know the infected person is most contagious when the initial blister appears. Unfortunately, the virus can be transmitted for at least a week before any symptoms appear and possibly for several months after signs of active infection have disappeared.

There is at present no vaccine to prevent HSV infection. There is no cure currently available either, although new classes of antiviral drugs such as acyclovir and vidarabine provide some pain relief and appear to shorten the duration of the primary infection. By promoting quicker healing, they also may shorten the period of contagion. These drugs, however, have not been recommended for routine use in young children. Doctors are concerned that they not be overutilized, especially without proven benefit, lest they create resistant strains of HSV. There are various other medications your doctor may prescribe such as viscous lidocaine (Xylocaine) that can be used to dull the pain of mouth ulcers in older children. These anesthetic preparations are applied directly to the blisters. Caution should be exercised when treating young children since the local anesthesia may create swallowing difficulties.

Mononucleosis

Mononucleosis is known as the "kissing disease." Many teenagers ask, "Is it mono?" worrying that they may have gotten the virus from a boyfriend or girlfriend. Younger children can also get mononucleosis, but usually they are not very sick and may have no symptoms at all.

Typically a child or teenager with mononucleosis is tired, frequently *very* tired. He complains of a sore throat and a headache and will have enlarged lymph nodes under his chin, neck, or armpits. His abdomen may be tender due to an enlargement of the spleen or liver. About twenty percent of mono patients develop a fine red rash over the chest, back, and abdomen that does not itch. (This rash, however, may be made more prominent by antibiotics mistakenly prescribed for the sore throat.) For a few patients mononucleosis may be more severe and prolonged, sometimes lasting for months. When the illness lingers a long time, a child may become quite depressed, and this possibility should be discussed early in the course of the illness.

There are some complications that may make mononucleosis more serious than it usually is. One is hepatitis, an inflammation of the liver that is characterized by jaundice (yellow skin), dark urine, and light-colored stools. Very occasionally the sore throat accompanying mononucleosis may be severe enough to cause swelling that requires hospital observation or medication with cortisone. Hospitalization may also be required if the virus affects the nervous system in such a way that a child has difficulty breathing. Luckily, these complications are very rare.

Although the diagnosis of mononucleosis is usually suggested by the symptoms, it may be confirmed by a blood test. The Epstein-Barr virus, which causes mononucleosis, can be distinguished from other organisms such as cytomegalovirus and *Toxoplasma* that cause illnesses indistinguishable from mononucleosis. People who have not had a specific laboratory diagnosis may mistakenly believe they have had mono more than once. The Epstein-Barr virus remains in the body in latent form after the initial infection, but except for rare and unusual situations in which it could reemerge, true mononucleosis is a one-time illness.

The mononucleosis virus is passed from person to person by contact with infected body fluids. Kissing, drinking from the same cup or straw, and sharing food are the most common means of transmission. Mononucleosis can also be transmitted through blood transfusions. It is difficult to predict when an exposed youngster may show signs of illness, since there is a long and variable incubation period of twenty to sixty days. A child may be contagious as long as the symptoms persist, but some youngsters may carry the virus in their throats for several months after they appear to have recovered from the illness; during this time they remain contagious and therefore capable of infecting their friends.

There is no specific treatment for this viral illness other than comforting the youngster. Most children will seek bed rest without any coaxing. As they recover and try to resume their full activities, they may temporarily relapse and require more rest than they anticipated. The sore throat can be treated with acetaminophen or the doctor may prescribe a stronger pain medication. Cool fluids rather than solid foods are appreciated. Occasionally cortisone may be prescribed if the tonsils are very large or if a child is very ill. There is no need for a special diet unless the illness is complicated by hepatitis. Since mononucleosis can be a long illness, it is also important to make plans for school and other commitments. Arrangements must be made for safe contact with friends and reasonable precautions taken to prevent the spread of the virus. If the spleen is very enlarged it may be necessary to curtail vigorous physical activities such as football or hockey. Depression and headache may be part of the illness, or a psychological consequence of its being so prolonged. It is important to reassure youngsters that their recovery will eventually be complete.

If "Is it mono?" is the first question kids ask, "When can I go back to school?" is the second. Returning to school generally depends on how the youngster feels. When his fever is gone, his throat is improved, and he can get through the day without a nap, he should be ready to return to school. But the strain of school or homework may be too much for a while. Often his schedule needs to be modified for a few weeks. The social calendar may be on hold even longer!

Fifth Disease (SLAPPED CHEEKS)

A little-known disease that is often diagnosed by exclusion, fifth disease received its name by being the fifth childhood virus simulating measles to be described. Its cause has recently been identified as a parvovirus. This very mild illness begins with the appearance of bright-red cheeks, which look as though they have been slapped. Many children get bright-red cheeks when they have a fever. However, the child with fifth disease may not have a fever, or if he does, it may be very slight. A fine red rash that does not itch soon appears on the arms, chest, back and buttocks. As the rash fades, it has a lacy appearance. A source of confusion and frustration is that the rash lingers and often comes and goes over a period of three weeks. Its reappearance is often precipitated by sunlight, changes in temperature, or trauma to the skin. The child does not seem particularly ill during this time.

This disease is probably transmitted from child to child through saliva or nasal discharge; the incubation period is four to six days. Unlike chicken pox, measles, and many other viral childhood illnesses, it does not seem to be highly contagious.

There is no specific treatment for fifth disease. The sick child usually feels fine or he may have a very slight fever and be a little cranky. Once again, this is a mild illness that resolves itself with time and patience.

Roseola

This mild childhood illness, which usually occurs between the ages of six and twenty-one months, is always a cause of great parental concern because the child's fever is often the highest it has ever been—103 to 105. Moreover, although the child may be irritable, no other signs of illness are evident, and there are no other clues to tell us what is going on for three to four days. Then the fever suddenly drops, the child is cool, and a fine, light-red rash appears on the face and chest. The rash usually spreads over the body and disappears within a day or two. Often the rash is so light that it is barely noticeable.

Children with roseola often look remarkably well, despite the initial high fever. We frequently see such children in the office during the early stage of the illness, rule out other illnesses such as an ear infection or tonsilitis, offer some reassurance, and send the family home to await the rash. But we cannot be sure of the diagnosis until the rash appears. Those children who are prone to having seizures with high temperatures may well have one during the early hours of this illness. Such a seizure should be reported to your child's doctor.

It is as yet unclear how roseola is spread. The incubation period is five to fifteen days. The period of contagion is also unclear but probably four or five days, beginning a day before the onset of the fever.

There is no specific treatment for this illness. Toddlers often feel fine except for their fever and may want to run about and play outside. The fever may respond somewhat to acetaminophen and lukewarm baths. Most children will welcome cool fluids and a cozy lap.

Bacterial Infections

When a child comes to the office with an earache, a sore throat, a bad cough suggestive of pneumonia, or an unusually swollen "insect bite," we know that a bacterial infection may be the cause of the problem. Although some bacteria seem to cause trouble only in specific parts of the body, most are capable of causing widespread infection. Identifying the particular bacterium involved (by taking a sample from the infected area and growing it in a laboratory culture) helps us decide how to treat the illness. When the area of infection is not accessible for a culture to be taken without undue trauma, as in the case of pneumonia, we may have to use other clues and diagnostic tools such as x-rays or blood tests to determine whether treatment with antibiotics is likely to be helpful. In other situations, such as ear infections, we have to rely on knowing which bacteria most frequently cause ear infections as well as the type of germ most prevalent in the community at the moment.

It is important to determine, if possible, precisely which bacterium is causing an infection since most bacterial infections can be eradicated if the proper antibiotic is selected. The number of useful antibiotics has increased greatly since the introduction of sulfa and penicillin fifty years ago. However, it is equally important that antibiotics not be used improperly or indiscriminately. It is now known that bacteria can become resistant to particular antibiotics, rendering them useless for treatment. Antibiotics, like other medicines, can cause unpleasant side effects as well, ranging from diarrhea and yeast infections to severe allergic reactions. (They do not, however, create any kind of weakness in immunity or alter the body's inherent ability to combat infection.) Some antibiotics should not be given to children, so don't borrow pills from friends, and when traveling abroad, don't use antibiotics that are commonly sold without prescription.

Enteric Infections

An enteric infection is one that is caused by bacteria that commonly exist as normal flora in the intestines such as *Escherichia, Klebsiella,* and *Proteus,* but are capable of causing illness elsewhere in the body.

Enteric infections in newborns are very serious. These bacteria can cause such life-threatening illnesses as meningitis, an infection of the membrane that covers the spinal cord and brain, and septicemia, an infection in the bloodstream. An infant with an enteric infection is very ill indeed. He may have a fever, be very irritable, too weak to nurse, and so lethargic that he resembles a floppy rag doll. In the case of meningitis, the soft spot on the top of the head (the fontanel) may feel very tight and full.

How an infant gets infected is not always clear. He may acquire the bacteria from his mother during birth or from other babies in the nursery. Nursery personnel are therefore rightly insistent that nurses as well as visitors wash their hands before handling a newborn.

The incubation period varies according to which bacterium is involved, and an infected infant is capable of excreting contagious bacteria in his stool for up to a week after treatment is begun.

Enteric infections in newborn infants are treated with antibiotics given intravenously in the hospital for ten days to three weeks, depending on the nature of the organism involved and the severity of the illness.

Enteric bacteria can also cause mild to severe diarrhea in people of all ages who are exposed to strains that are not part of their normal flora. *E. coli* in particular can cause a severe epidemic diarrhea seen in infants as well as travelers' diarrhea. The latter is particularly difficult to avoid because the bacteria can be present on food, utensils, towels, and money (paper and coins). Though washing hands with soap and water may help, most preventive measures are relatively impractical, and most medications against travelers' diarrhea are unsafe for young children. Enteric bacteria are also a common cause of urinary tract infections because the exits from the urinary tract and intestine are so close together (see chapter on urinary-tract disorders).

Hemophilus influenzae (TYPE B)

Hemophilus influenzae is the name of a bacterium, normally a harmless resident of the nose and throat, that occasionally causes a serious disease, especially in young children. It is not "the flu," which is caused by a virus. *Hemophilus influenzae* (sometimes called "*H. flu*" just to confuse everyone further) is responsible for about 12,000 cases of meningitis a year in this country; five percent of the cases are fatal, and about twenty-five percent result in neurological or hearing damage. Other serious deep-tissue infections caused by *H.*

flu are periorbital cellulitis (an infection of the skin around the eye; see chapter on eye problems), orbital cellulitis (an infection of the eye itself), epiglottitis (an infection of the protective "lid" of the windpipe), osteomyelitis (an infection of the bone), septicemia (a blood infection), and pneumonia.

Infants and young children three months to four years old are most susceptible to these serious infections. The bacteria are spread from child to child by contact with infected nasal mucus and sputum. Hemophilus infections, therefore, occur more frequently and earlier in day-care settings where many young children are together. The incubation period is thought to be less than ten days. A child with this type of infection is contagious as long as the bacteria are growing in his respiratory tract. Infected children are treated with intravenous antibiotics, but cease to be contagious only after receiving an additional medication to curtail the "carrier state."

A child with *H. flu* meningitis may pass the germ to another child, but the second child may not necessarily get meningitis. He may get another severe form of *H. flu* infection, such as epiglottitis, or something mild, such as an ear infection.

When hemophilus meningitis, epiglottitis, or orbital cellulitis is diagnosed in the community, we get many calls from parents asking if there is a way to prevent their exposed child from getting the disease. Depending on the closeness of contact and the age of the exposed child, antibiotics may be advised, to prevent and to keep him from unwittingly spreading the disease. The exposed child's doctor or a public health physician should be contacted to determine the proper course to take.

A vaccine against *Hemophilus influenzae* has been released for general use and is recommended by the American Academy of Pediatrics for children between the ages of eighteen months and five years. Babies who have had hemophilus meningitis or epiglottitis should still get the vaccine at eighteen months, since a child can get this disease more than once. Unfortunately, the vaccine now available is not effective in younger children and therefore not useful for those at highest risk. It is also not a hundred percent effective in blocking the disease. Nevertheless, it seems a good preventive step, especially for children in day-care settings. We are waiting for a more effective vaccine.

Pneumococcal Infections

The pneumococcus is one of the organisms most often responsible for acute ear infections in children. It also frequently causes such diseases as sinusitis, pneumonia, and meningitis. In children between one month and two years of age it is the most common cause of septicemia (bacterial infection in the bloodstream). Very young children, children with conditions such as sickle cell disease, children who have had their spleens removed, and children receiving cortisone treatment or chemotherapy are at greatest risk of developing pneumococcal infections. Fortunately a vaccine is available that offers some protection to children over the age of two who are at particularly increased risk of pneumococcal infections.

The pneumococcus may be found in the respiratory tract as part of its normal flora without causing illness. Some strains are more likely to cause illness than others, but exactly why one child stays healthy while another gets sick remains a mystery. Because the bacterium is present in nasal mucus and sputum, children can pass it to one another by coughing, sneezing, and sharing contaminated toys and bottles.

The incubation period depends on the type of infection the pneumococcus causes. It may be as brief as one to three days or as long as a month. The contagious period continues as long as living bacteria are present in the secretions of the nose and throat.

Most pneumococcal infections respond to treatment with the appropriate antibiotic within twenty-four hours. A child with a pneumococcal infection of the ear or the sinuses who feels well enough to return to day-care or to school should be able to do so within twenty-four to forty-eight hours after beginning treatment. If a child develops a more serious deep-tissue infection such as meningitis, the recovery period will be longer (see chapter on fever for full discussion of meningitis).

Staphylococcal Infections

Staphylococcal bacteria are found on the skin and in the nose of about thirty percent of all healthy children and adults. Normal flora again! But when the skin is broken by a cut, for example, or a bug bite, or when another infection weakens a child's resistance, these otherwise innocuous bacteria may cause trouble. The trouble can take many forms including skin infections such as abscesses (boils), or impetigo (a collection of pus-filled blisters that dry to form yellow crusts), septicemia (an infection in the bloodstream), pneumonia, sinusitis, and (rarely) meningitis. Staphylococcal bacteria are easily passed from child to child by contact with an infected area, such as an impetigo sore, or with nasal discharge, as in the case of sinusitis. The incubation period is one to ten days, and the child with a staphylococcal infection remains contagious until all bacteria are eradicated, usually twenty-four to forty-eight hours after treatment is begun. Staphylococcal infections can be treated effectively with appropriate antibiotics. Resistant strains exist, however, and these require a special antibiotic.

Staphylococcal food poisoning is caused by a toxin produced by the bacteria. The staphylococci may be on the skin of a food handler or in spoiled food. The symptoms of food poisoning are primarily vomiting and abdominal discomfort. The incubation period ranges from half an hour to seven hours. There is no specific treatment for staphylococcal food poisoning. A child who is ill with food poisoning usually begins to feel much better once he has stopped vomiting.

Streptococcal Infections

Streptococcal bacteria can cause many kinds of infections including ear infections, sinusitis, septicemia, endocarditis (an infection of the inner lining of the heart), and skin infections like impetigo. But the tonsils and the throat are the most frequent sites of strep infections (see chapter on sore throat). Strep throat is most commonly seen in children over the age of three. The bacteria are present in saliva and are spread when children cough and share straws or drinking glasses. The incubation period is two to five days. The child is contagious until he has been treated for twenty-four hours with antibiotics, or in the case of an untreated child until the symptoms have abated and several weeks have elapsed. Treating a child with the appropriate antibiotic is by far the better course, since treatment will reduce his chances of spreading the disease and ensure a quicker recovery. Furthermore, antibiotics will often eliminate other complications, such as a throat abscess, and may significantly reduce the possibility of the child developing rheumatic fever, a rare complication of strep throat, which may affect the joints, heart, skin, nervous system, and general well-being of a child.

Scarlet fever is another manifestation of strep throat. This illness, which does not always accompany strep throat, is distinguished by a fever, sore throat, and a very light red rough rash over the entire chest. The rash usually emerges two to three days after the onset of the sore throat. Scarlet fever is not a separate illness but rather the body's reaction to a strep infection. If a parent is unaware that her child has a strep throat, the development of the rash associated with scarlet fever will alert her to this possibility and the need for treatment.

Impetigo is another commonly encountered infection that can be caused by streptococci. The bacteria are easily spread by contact with the sores or with nasal mucus. An open wound exposed to the very streptococci that make up part of the normal skin flora may also become infected. The incubation period for impetigo is about ten days, and the child is contagious until he has been treated for forty-eight hours.

When one or two minor sores are present it may be sufficient to treat them with a topical antibiotic such as Bacitracin. However, if there are many sores, an oral antibiotic should be taken. In any case, after a bout of infection, it is wise to use an antibacterial soap (pHisoDerm, Hibiclens) for several weeks to clean the skin.

One rare complication of strep impetigo is glomerulonephritis, a serious kidney ailment, usually signaled by brown-red urine. It is unclear whether or not early treatment of impetigo can prevent the development of glomerulonephritis.

A streptococcal infection may recur despite treatment, and the course of medication may have to be repeated.

These common bacterial infections become familiar, though unwanted, guests in most households with young children. We expect to encounter these microbes as soon as children begin to play together in large groups, whether in day-care centers at six months old or in kindergarten at age five.

Parasitic Infections

Despite the fact that public health measures have substantially reduced the incidence of parasitic disease in the developed world, our children are still likely to encounter one or more of these infestations in the course of their normal activities. Parasites thrive in crowded conditions, and the number of young children attending preschool and day-care has increased significantly over the past decade. The amount of time they spend there has also increased—and so has the frequency with which we are seeing certain common parasites such as pinworms, giardia, head lice, and skin mites. As more people travel abroad, we can expect to see more and more parasites that were once considered exotic. And as more people take to the outdoors and our national parks and rivers get increasingly contaminated, parasitic infections such as giardia become an all too frequent hazard of the camper's adventure.

Giardiasis

Once rarely seen in this country, today the parasite *Giardia lamblia* immediately comes to mind when a parent reports persistent diarrhea or loose, foul-smelling stools, diminished appetite, and cramping abdominal pains. Parents often are surprised when we ask whether they have been camping in the mountains recently or whether any other children at the day-care center have similar symptoms. Giardia are often acquired from contaminated water. The water in many freshwater lakes and rivers is unsafe for drinking, and campers are well advised to purify the water they intend to drink by using chemical tablets or by boiling it for two minutes. This parasite makes its home in the host's intestine, and the eggs and cysts that contaminate the stool can be passed to another person if hands are not carefully washed after going to the bathroom or before preparing food. Giardia can be transmitted from infant to infant if caretakers fail to wash their hands after changing diapers or fail to keep changing tabies and potty chairs clean. The incubation period is usually one to four weeks. However, we have had families who harbored the parasite for five to six months before they noticed the signs of infection.

This disease is contagious as long as there are cysts in the stool. Sometimes these cysts disappear spontaneously, but treatment with an appropriate prescription medication is usually recommended in order to reduce the symptoms and prevent spread. Giardiasis may recur repeatedly and require several courses of treatment.

Pinworms

Most parents are truly horrified when they find little white, threadlike, wiggly worms around their child's rectum, in the bedding, or in underwear. While pinworms can cause some irritation and itching which may interrupt a child's sleep, they are harmless and do not lead to illness. Even before these uninvited guests are discovered by a parent, the child usually complains of itching around the anus or vagina, which typically seems worse at night. Occasionally a child will complain of stomach cramps or wet his pants or his bed.

If you are on a search for worms, the best time to

examine your child's bottom is during the night or in the wee hours of the morning. If there is any doubt, the tiny eggs can be collected by applying cellulose tape, sticky side down, to the skin of the rectal area. The tape is then attached to a slide and examined under the microscope.

Pinworms hatch in the intestines, but they emerge from the anus to lay their eggs outside the body. The infection spreads when these eggs are passed on, by hand contact or in food, and then ingested by a new victim. For example, an infected child who touches his bottom and inadvertently gets the eggs on his hands can pass them to his playmates, so children should be instructed to wash their hands after using the bathroom. People taking care of infants should also be sure to wash their hands after changing diapers and before preparing food. And again, clean changing tables and potty chairs will help prevent the spread of this uncomfortable problem.

When the diagnosis is confirmed, oral medication, either liquid or chewable tablets, is given for one to three days to kill the worms. Some abdominal discomfort and red stools may occur, depending on the medication used. Worms may continue to emerge from the anus for some time after treatment has ended. Some physicians recommend treating all family members, while others prefer to begin with only those known to be infected. And then you have the additional joy of cleaning the toilets with disinfectant and thoroughly laundering towels and bedding. It is most important to reassure an infested child that lots of people get pinworms, that it's not the result of being "dirty," and that the medication will definitely make those worms go away.

Pediculosis (LICE)

Many a parent lovingly combing her child's fine hair has been horrified to see tiny live insects crawling around the scalp. These are lice, tiny insects who lay their eggs wherever there are hair follicles. On closer inspection one may see the eggs (nits), tiny brown (full) or white (empty) sacks that surround the hair follicles near the scalp and stick tightly to the child's hair. These same bugs and nits may also be found on the eyebrows and eyelashes, on body hair, and on clothing. But by far the most prevalent are head lice—the scourge of schools!

Head lice are not an indication of lack of cleanliness. Infestation spreads easily among children, especially if they share combs, clothes, pillows, or hats. Lice can survive away from the body at room temperature for ten days, so they can also infest rugs at school and bedding at home.

An itchy scalp is the most common symptom of head lice; small, red bumps found along the hairline and behind the child's ears are other signs of lice. Finding lice or nits makes the diagnosis certain. The initial treatment consists of a thorough shampooing with over-the-counter products like A-200, Rid, or Pronto or with prescription preparations such as Nix or Kwell, which are usually successful in ridding the scalp of these obnoxious visitors. Most preparations require a second treatment one week after the first to kill any surviving eggs. In addition to the shampoo treatment, live nits must be removed daily with a fine-toothed comb. Wrapping the head in a towel soaked in white vinegar may help break down the eggs' protective coating, making the combing process easier. Be very careful to keep these medications out of the eyes.

All combs, brushes, barettes, and the like must be washed in hot water mixed with the same shampoo or rinse used on the child's hair. Lice and eggs are killed when exposed to ten minutes or more of heat. Therefore, all bedding and clothing worn within forty-eight hours of the first treatment should be washed in the washing machine, and dried in the dryer on the hot cycle. Dry cleaning and vacuuming are also effective, as is placing clothing in a sealed plastic bag for fourteen days.

Children can return to school the morning after their first treatment. All family members should be treated or observed closely for infestation. Recurrences are all too common, and though head lice cause no serious disease, they are annoying.

Scabies

Another troublesome parasite is *Sarcoptes scabiei,* a tiny mite that burrows under the skin, causing a very irritating rash. In fact, it itches like crazy. The rash sometimes looks like a squiggly line and can be found anywhere, although in young children it usually appears on the chest, back, and limbs. In older children it is found between the fingers, over the wrist and ankles, at the belt line, and on the chest. Scabies is a great masquerader; the rash may look like tiny red bumps or small scabs created by scratching. Diagnosis can be confirmed by isolating the tiny mite.

These parasites are passed from person to person by direct skin contact. They can also travel on clothing though they will not survive longer than four days away from the body. The incubation period is two to six weeks for a first infection and one to four days in the case of a recurrence.

If the area of infection is small, an initial treatment with crotamitin cream (Eurax) may be effective. If not, an insecticide lotion such as lindane (Kwell) is applied at night to the entire body (except the face) and washed off in the morning.

This treatment should be repeated one week later. We advise treating all family members at the same time. Babies less than six months old can be treated with ten-percent sulfur in petrolatum instead of Kwell, which may be toxic at this age. All clothing worn within forty-eight hours of treatment should be washed and put in a hot dryer. Clothing that cannot be washed should be kept in a sealed plastic bag for two weeks. Some confusion may result from the fact that the rash can persist for two to three weeks after all the mites have been killed. But there is no reason to worry—the pests are gone.

Rashes and Other Skin Problems

Skin problems occur for a great variety of reasons, so they are sometimes difficult to diagnose. While most are not serious and cause only minor discomfort, they may offer valuable clues to other health problems.

Skin rashes pose a particular challenge to parents and doctors alike. Parents often find it difficult to tell how serious a rash is and whether a visit to the doctor is necessary. Determining the cause of a mysterious outbreak over the telephone tests the parents' powers of description and the doctor's diagnostic skills, for there are many different kinds of skin rashes, ranging from the trivial to the serious. Some rashes are the result of exposure to a substance the skin regards as foreign or irritating, such as poison ivy. Others are signs of a bacterial or viral infection, such as those that appear with scarlet fever and chicken pox. Still others are indications of a fungal infection like ringworm or athlete's foot. Tiny purple dots may be seen on a child's face after vomiting or on the arm after a tight squeeze, but these are usually a normal response to excessive pressure on the skin. Sometimes a variety of rashes can coexist, making diagnosis even more difficult.

In trying to find the underlying reason for a rash, your doctor will want to know not only what the rash looks like, but also when and where it first appeared, how it progressed, and whether or not there are other associated symptoms such as fever, itching, or pain. While a rash may not seem serious enough for an office visit, one good look can usually put an end to needless worry. In general, if a rash is not accompanied by other signs of illness and is causing no pain or itching, it may be observed at home for several days. Many rashes disappear without treatment when the irritant causing it is removed. Other rashes will linger, and your child should certainly be examined by his doctor if a rash fails to clear up in a week, or if it recurs.

Skin Conditions in Newborns

There are a number of innocent rashes that may appear during the first few months of life and then clear up spontaneously. Close to fifty percent of all healthy babies develop erythema toxicum, a rash that resembles flea bites. It shows up a few days after birth and comes and goes for a week or two. The small bumps, which may be raised, are red, often with slightly white centers. Babies do not seem at all bothered by the rash which travels around the body, appearing perhaps on the face in the morning, the belly at noon, and the arms at night.

Slightly fewer than half the newborns we see have a condition called milia, tiny white dots on the nose, forehead, and cheeks that are the result of an overabundance of normal skin secretions. These dots disappear spontaneously a few weeks after birth.

Infant acne may appear on a baby's face about two weeks after birth and often lasts from one to three months, sometimes longer. It is thought to be related to an infant's exposure to maternal hormones and has no relationship to diet or adult acne. Although dismaying to parents, no specific treatment is needed for it though we sometimes suggest gently wiping the baby's face with a soothing lotion such as Cetaphil.

Heat rash or prickly heat is also common in newborns. The small pores leading from the sweat glands to the skin surface are still developing, so that when a baby is overheated and perspires, moisture is retained within the skin causing tiny red bumps that most often appear on the chest, face, or upper back, or in the creases of the neck and armpits. Removing excess clothing and keeping the baby in a cool place will usually cause the rash to disappear.

The most common type of rash seen in infants is diaper rash. Typically, the red, dry, flat rash confined to the diaper area is due to irritation of the skin by urine and stool. Ammonia in the urine causes a chemical burn of the skin. Frequently, the diaper itself, or the perfumes that it contains, may irritate the baby's skin. This is true of both paper and cloth diapers.

We recommend that diapers be washed in mild soap and rinsed well. If ammonia is the problem, adding half a cup of white vinegar to the rinse water may help. Diaper liners are also available to absorb excess ammonia. Soakers can be used in place of plastic covers. Common diaper rash can be treated with soothing ointments such as zinc oxide, Desitin, A and D Ointment, Eucerin, or Caldesene. Exposing the baby's bottom to the air is often the best treatment and talc-free powder can be used to absorb excess moisture. If there are raw areas, blisters, peeling, or bleeding, a visit to the doctor may be necessary.

A simple diaper rash can become infected by yeast because yeast organisms like moist, warm environments. Skin infections from yeast usually look bright red and sometimes have a white cast. There is often a rim of small, separate bumps at the edge of the red area or running through it. This rash usually appears around the anus, penis, or vaginal area. Some babies will also develop thrush, a yeast infection that causes white patches inside the mouth and cheeks. A yeast infection often follows treatment with antibiotics. Newborns can acquire yeast infection during birth, and some babies get it for no apparent reason. It usually clears up after two to three weeks of treatment with nystatin or another antiyeast preparation.

Cradle cap is a form of seborrhea that appears on an infant's scalp. This same condition, in which shedded skin is trapped in oils near the hair follicles, is responsible for itchy dandruff in older children and adults. Babies can get seborrhea on the forehead, in the eyebrows, behind the ears, on the cheeks—wherever there are hair follicles. If seborrhea causes irritation, the skin looks red. Otherwise it may look scaly, yellowish, and greasy. In general, seborrhea is only a cosmetic problem and requires no treatment. Washing the baby's scalp and face with an unscented mild soap every two to four days should help. If it doesn't, try applying vegetable oil to the scalp half an hour before shampooing. After the oil has been absorbed, gently loosen the scales by brushing with a hairbrush or toothbrush or by rubbing with your fingertips. If this treatment does not work, a mild antidandruff shampoo without tar may be tried. If facial skin becomes very irritated, Cetaphil lotion can be applied once or twice a day. If a baby is really uncomfortable or if the skin behind the ears develops cracks, hydrocortisone cream may be applied to the affected areas twice a day, but only for a few days, unless your doctor directs otherwise. If there is wetness or oozing behind the ears, an antibacterial ointment like Bacitracin can be used.

No discussion of skin conditions common to newborn babies would be complete without a mention of birthmarks. Many, many babies are born with birthmarks. Some of them look somewhat like rashes. They may be red, blue, black, or tan, flat or raised. Most are of no significance, and many disappear during childhood.

Parents are often the first to notice the flat, red marks frequently seen at the nape of a baby's neck or on his eyelids, nose, and forehead. These are macular hemangiomas, also known as "storkbites." Occasionally, a large macular hemangioma may be part of a more serious condition involving internal disorders. Your doctor will advise you if your baby's birthmark is of this nature. Generally, "storkbites" are of no significance and usually disappear between a child's first and third birthday. Equally innocuous is the raised reddish-purple raspberry-shaped mark known as a capillary hemangioma. This common birthmark, which may be anywhere on the body, usually first appears several weeks after birth. It often begins as a small collection of purple dots or a white ring, then gradually grows into a raised berrylike bump reaching its maximum size at about nine months. Most capillary hemangiomas gradually recede over the next year or two.

Infants with dark skin are frequently born with one or more rather large bluish-purple marks known as mongolian spots. They are generally on the buttocks or back, but may appear anywhere on the body. Parents are often concerned because the marks resemble bruises, but they are of no consequence and usually fade as the child grows.

Light-brown areas called café-au-lait spots are commonly seen at birth and are of no significance unless there are more than four of them. Moles are also usually harmless unless they are very large, cover an entire limb or body part (such as an ear, foot, or eyelid), have an unusual texture or color, or are changing. The baby's doctor will usually notice moles, but parents should also point them out. One other common mark seen on newborns is a sebaceous nevus, a shiny, round, orange spot usually found on a baby's scalp. Although it does not usually cause problems during childhood, it may eventually have to be removed since some of these birthmarks have shown a tendency to become malignant later on.

Although birthmarks come in a very wide variety, the important thing to remember is that most of the common kinds are harmless. Many disappear by themselves leaving barely a trace while others remain throughout life—spots of distinction.

Red Patches

Parents are sometimes alarmed when they notice red areas on their child's skin. Red patches can show up on any part of the body—on the cheeks or next to the lips, on the arms or behind the knees—and can be caused by many different things. One of the more common conditions, eczema, may be caused by dry skin, often together with an allergic reaction to a food or to some substance in the child's environment such as fabric, laundry soap, fabric softeners, and clothing snaps that contain nickel. Initially these patchy areas may be red, dry, and itchy and often appear circular. However, with prolonged scratching the skin may thicken and the dry area may become weepy and infected. Children with eczema often look uncomfortable and act irritable. A baby may have very red, irritated cheeks that he tries to scratch by rubbing on bedding, toys, or the floor.

Many parents find that when they remove specific foods or materials from the child's environment, such as wool, chemicals, and dyes, the eczema clears up. Some children seem to outgrow their eczema, while others are plagued by it all their lives.

In treating eczema, first find out what might be causing the allergic reaction and remove it, if at all possible. Because water dries the skin you should reduce the number of baths your child takes to one a week, and eliminate harsh, scented soaps and detergents (including so-called "baby products") when bathing your child. Instead, use a cleansing soap or lotion such as Cetaphil and a dye-free, unscented moisturizing cream such as Lubriderm, Eucerin, or Complex 15. Nails should be cut short to minimize the possibility of infection due to scratching. Since warmth aggravates the symptoms of eczema, children should not be overdressed or bundled too tightly at night. When dealing with severe eczema, hydrocortisone creams are usually applied two to three times a day for two to three weeks. If the skin becomes infected from scratching, oral antibiotics and antihistamines may be given.

Eczema can mimic the appearance of many other skin problems. In infants a form of eczema known as nummular eczema takes on a circular patchy appearance and can be confused with ringworm. Light-colored, dry, cornmeal-textured, round patches on the baby's stomach, back, and extremities suggest nummular eczema. These patches do not have a raised border like the rash of ringworm and, although the spots may appear in several places, they do not get bigger as do ringworm lesions. Nummular eczema is almost never seen in the diaper area. It can be treated with the same measures outlined above for eczema.

If the rash doesn't look quite like eczema, it could *be* ringworm. Ringworm does not always appear in the shape of a ring nor is it caused by a worm. It is a fungal condition that starts as a small red circular patch. As the spot enlarges, the center returns to normal, leaving a bumpy raised border that is the characteristic red and scaly "ring." The infection can also cause affected areas to lose their pigmentation—usually only temporarily. Ringworm is mildly contagious and is spread by direct contact. It can be treated with over-the-counter antifungal creams, such as Micatin or Desenex, or, if it fails to respond, with stronger prescription creams. It may take several weeks for ringworm to clear up.

Eczema can affect any area of the body, including the feet, where it is sometimes mistaken for athlete's foot. The distinction may be tricky, but it is important since the two conditions should be treated differently. When the soles of the feet are cracked, red, and peeling, the cause is apt to be eczema. It may be a reaction to sweat and shows as painful patches that may even bleed. Rubber sneakers prevent moisture from evaporating, so you may find that switching your child to sandals or leather shoes will help. Wearing absorbent cotton sweat socks and using foot powders are also effective. Sometimes it is necessary to treat severe ezcema of the feet with hydrocortisone cream.

If the skin between the toes is cracked, your child probably *does* have athlete's foot, a fungal infection that can be picked up anywhere, especially where many people share humid conditions, as in locker rooms. It can usually be treated successfully with antifungal medications available without prescription, such as Micatin, Tinactin, and Desenex, but if the infection persists, prescription medications may be required. Sometimes children with athlete's foot will have tiny red bumps on the sides of their fingers. This is called an id reaction and is of no great significance. A rash similar to that of athlete's foot can occur in any skin fold where moisture tends to collect, such as the neck, armpits, or crotch (the famous jock itch). Treatment for any fungal condition should be continued for two weeks or more after the rash has cleared up to prevent an immediate recurrence.

Two other conditions that may show as red patches deserve mention. Tinea capitis, a fungal infection, causes a rash on the scalp that is often red and scaly. It may ooze as little pustules open and drain. An affected child's doctor may treat this infection with griseofulvin, an oral antibiotic that must be taken for several weeks. Pityriasis rosea, another red patchy skin eruption, qualifies as one of our mystery rashes. It tends to appear on the chest and back, first as a mixture of coin-size patches and smaller spots. The rash generally does not itch a great deal and children who have it are not sick. Gradually, one spot may enlarge and become prominent. When it is typical, the rest of the rash tends to align in a "Christmas tree" pattern on the back suggestive of branches. It goes away in three to six weeks without treatment.

Red Rashes

Fine red or pink rashes that appear as sheets of small bumps on the surface of the skin are most often caused by one of the many infectious diseases so common in childhood. Such rashes usually don't itch, although there are some glaring exceptions! Most of the viral rashes blanch—that is, they turn pale when pressed with a finger. A rash that doesn't blanch with pressure could represent a more serious problem and should be reported to your child's doctor. Very rarely, nonblanching pinpoint purple rashes come from microscopic bleeding into the skin or from clumps of bacteria that escape small blood vessels and lodge in the skin. Most of the time, small nonblanching dots are a part of harmless viral illnesses, but it is best that your child's doctor make this distinction.

Dots due to viral infections may itch some, but if your child is scratching furiously, think of scabies, a contagious rash caused by a burrowing insect. This mite likes to travel beneath the skin, so the dots may group in small lines. They may also be in patches between the fingers or on the abdomen but usually not on the face. We dwell a bit more on scabies in the section on parasites. A prescription cream or lotion will take care of the problem.

A far more common cause of red dots is heat rash, also known as prickly heat; see the discussion above under "Skin Conditions in Newborns."

Sometimes, larger areas of skin turn red. The cheeks may blush for days during a viral illness called fifth disease. A rough red rash of the chest, face, and tongue may accompany strep throat and scarlet fever. Some medications or embarrassing situations can cause a temporary flush to the cheeks.

One special, annoying rash that can cause red, inflamed skin, as well as crusting, blistering, and weeping is that which results from exposure to poison oak or poison ivy. Here, the oils produced by the plants cause a chemical and allergic burnlike reaction. A clue to the cause of these rashes is their appearance on areas of the skin not covered by clothing. You can get a rash from direct contact with the plants, from oil on the fur of animals, or from clothing or equipment that has touched the plants. Washing exposed skin with strong soap and lots of warm water will remove the irritating oil. The key to the success of this measure seems to be time; clean your child's skin immediately if you suspect he has been exposed.

If a rash develops in spite of all precautions, it may appear to spread and get worse over several hours or days. This reaction is almost always caused by late-developing symptoms, not by further exposure to the poisonous plants. Touching the rash itself will not cause a secondary rash elsewhere.

Treatment includes applying cool wet compresses or

giving cool baths containing colloidal oatmeal (follow package directions) or baking soda (½ cup for a shallow bath). Calamine lotion (not Caladryl) or a mild hydrocortisone cream or lotion may relieve itching. If itching continues, an oral antihistamine may be given. If these measures don't help, your child's doctor may prescribe an oral cortisone medication such as prednisone.

It is important to remember that if poison oak and poison ivy are burned, their noxious oil can be carried through the air in the smoke. Anyone who might be sensitive, child or adult, should certainly be protected from such smoke. If the oil lands on the skin, it can cause the same rash; if it is breathed in, it can cause irritation of the respiratory tract, including acute wheezing.

White Patches

There are many causes of loss of skin pigment, and while this condition is usually nothing to worry about, it can be especially noticeable and disturbing when it happens to dark-skinned people. Some children are born with white patches, or vitiligo. If you see such marks, it is probably a good idea to point them out to your pediatrician, since he may not have noticed the spots, and they are occasionally significant. Some white patches in older children are the result of a chronic skin problem, like a fungal infection. Others, such as a scaly patchy lightening of the skin called pityriasis alba, are of unknown cause. Once pigment has disappeared, it may take months to return, even after the original problem has been solved.

A fungal infection known as tinea versicolor can cause patches of skin to lose their pigmentation. These light spots are more evident in the summer because they do not tan.

Tinea versicolor is a rash that is usually seen on the neck, arms, and upper back. The patches may be irregular in shape and have a slightly scaly light pink, tan, or white appearance. Sometimes this condition resolves with treatment, but it may take weeks or even months. Some people have found they can hasten the process by washing the affected areas weekly with an antidandruff shampoo. Even after adequate treatment, the condition often recurs.

Hives

Our exposé of the skin becomes increasingly colorful as we look at hives and similar skin reactions. Sometimes the red or white welts, bumps, and circular "bull's-eye" marks of hives may all be present at the same time. Hives can be caused by viruses or by a number of irritants or allergens including foods, plants, drugs, heat, and cold. If a child gets hives while on medication, the medicine should be stopped without delay and the doctor consulted. If hives are accompanied by wheezing, choking, or swelling of the mouth or throat, the child's doctor should be called *at once*.

Mild allergic reactions can be treated by removing the cause of the reaction, placing cool compresses on the rash, and giving oral antihistamine such as Benadryl or Atarax. Sometimes these medications are continued for several days after the exposure has ended because the reaction can come back. When a hivelike rash is thought to be due to a virus, treatment may not be necessary at all. The rash departs along with the virus.

Sunburn

In true, acute sunburn the skin will be bright red and red bumps may show up four to six hours after a child has been in the sun. Within a few hours, small fluid-filled blisters will appear under the skin. The child may be in pain for several hours, and acetaminophen can certainly be given. Within three to seven days the injured layers of skin usually begin to peel. Cool compresses and preparations such as an aloe vera lotion may be soothing. It is best not to use greasy ointments like petroleum jelly (Vaseline) since they retain heat and may cause the child to feel even more uncomfortable. You should also avoid anaesthetic products that contain benzocaine. Though these creams may provide temporary pain relief, they can be irritating and prolong recovery.

When a sunburn is accompanied by symptoms such as dizziness, nausea, or fever, your child's doctor should be notified.

Naturally, it is best to avoid sunburn altogether by limiting the time your child spends in the sun, especially between the hours of eleven a.m. and two p.m., when the sun's rays are most penetrating. You should use a sunscreen whenever you and your children plan to be outdoors for any length of time. A PABA-containing sunscreen rated 15 SPF or higher is appropriate for all ages, provided your child is not allergic to it. Sunscreens without PABA are also available. But even with sunscreens, excessive exposure to the sun should be avoided.

Dry Skin

That smooth perfect skin that a baby is born with is not immune to the stresses of the environment. Sunlight, water, and chemicals can dry a child's skin to the point where it feels rough and itches terribly. So many times we hear proud parents tell us they wash their baby from head to toe every day. These babies may look and smell beautiful, but their skin may not be so happy. When the skin is unable to retain adequate amounts of water, it dries out. Scratching often produces infection which compounds the problem. Although some dry skin conditions are inherited, the causes of dry skin are most often external, such as too-frequent bathing or too-intense sun-worshipping. There are also many ways to abuse the skin chemically, by using harsh soaps, detergents, bleaches, and fabric softeners.

A very common form of dry skin is an inherited condition called keratosis pilaris. The keratin or scaly layer of the skin builds up, producing a dry, rough rash, usually on the back of the arms, thighs, and buttocks. In younger children it may also appear on the cheeks. Teenagers endearingly refer to this condition as "chicken skin." Although this condition is usually less prominent in the summer, it is chronic and never completely goes away. Lubricating lotions, creams, and ointments may be helpful.

Excessive exposure to the sun can dry the skin, creating the need for frequent lubrication. Creams such as Eucerin, Lubriderm, Complex 15, and Keri are soothing and effective.

Some children's skin becomes dry and irritated simply from being exposed to water. Others have bad reactions to the chemicals found in household detergents. Many a lucky youngster is unable to wash dishes because the detergent irritates his hands or because extended exposure to water causes his skin to become chapped, cracked, and eventually infected. Creams such as the ones mentioned above will often provide relief.

Blisters and Boils

A great number of conditions can result in fluid-filled blisters on the skin. Some blisters open and drain, others crust over, and yet others do neither!

Individual blisters may be the result of swinging on the bars at the park, or wearing tight shoes. Intact blisters should be washed carefully. If the area around the blister becomes very red or the child develops a fever, the skin may be infected and the doctor should be called.

Blisters can also be caused by viruses. The herpes simplex virus, for example, causes the blisters we generally call "cold sores." (See chapter on infections.) Other examples are chicken pox and Coxsackie virus.

Another rash that may form blisters is caused by superficially infected skin, or impetigo. If a rash begins oozing a clear or golden fluid that subsequently forms a crust, it may be caused by bacteria, either by streptococci or staphylococci (see chapter on common infections). Impetigo may also infect skin without a rash, often beginning as a few crusty, oozing spots especially in the nostrils, on the face, or on the buttocks. If it is a discrete spot or two, impetigo can be controlled by using antibacterial soaps such as Dial, Betadine, pHisoDerm, or Hibiclens, and antibacterial ointments such as Polysporin or Bacitracin. But if it is extensive and if it is spreading, oral antibiotics are needed, because impetigo is very contagious and is spread by direct contact. Lesions should be covered so that children cannot give it to their playmates. The infection is contagious until antibiotics have been given for twenty-four to forty-eight hours. Serious kidney disease may occasionally result from untreated impetigo, so this condition should not be neglected. If a child who has had impetigo has red or brown urine the child's doctor should be told at once.

Blisters that appear to be filled with cloudy fluid (pus) and are surrounded by red, tender skin are actually boils. Boils are the result of a staphylococcal infection and may appear anywhere on the body. They can grown to be the size of a cherry pit or even a walnut and they are often very painful. Warm compresses applied three to four times a day will promote circulation and thus help the blister to rupture and the pus to drain. Once the boil drains, the skin around it should be kept very clean and an antibiotic ointment such as Polysporin or Bacitracin used for a few days. If the boil is unresponsive to this treatment or the child has a fever, your doctor may prescribe antibiotics. Occasionally a boil needs to be opened by the doctor to relieve the pain and control the infection.

Acne

Acne is a skin condition most often associated with normal adolescence, but it can occur earlier. The typical pimples of acne are the result of an inflammation of the sebaceous (oil) glands under the skin near hair follicles. Acne is related neither to uncleanliness nor directly to diet, although some people find that certain foods, such as chocolate, fat or nuts, seem to aggravate the condition.

Acne should be treated carefully to prevent scars. Frequent washing with anti-acne soaps and treatment with astringent lotions, or benzoyl peroxide creams or gels, can help reduce the severity of acne. If these products dry the skin excessively, they should be used only every second or third day. If acne is not controlled by these measures, your child's doctor may prescribe a drying medication such as antibiotic lotions or Retin-A cream, or oral antibiotics such as tetracycline. Be careful in using tetracycline and Retin-A in the summer, since they can both cause severe sunburns of the skin, and tetracycline can affect the nailbeds as well.

We urge parents not to accept disfiguring acne as "something we all go through." Proper treatment can control this problem until it subsides with adulthood.

Warts

Warts are small, rough, raised, flesh-colored flat growths on the surface of the skin. They are very common in childhood and can appear anywhere on the body but are most often seen on the hands, feet, and knees. They are caused by wart viruses and may spread slowly from site to site. Warts do not itch and are generally painless. However, when they occur on the soles of the feet, they can be very painful. If they are not causing pain, they should be left alone; they will eventually go away. Sometimes warts are treated with plasters (Mediplast) or acid liquids (Duofilm) to reduce their growth, but neither this treatment nor the removal of warts with liquid nitrogen guarantees that they won't return.

Multiple small wartlike bumps, usually on the chest or face, may be due to molluscum contagiosum, a mildly contagious disorder caused by a virus. This condition usually clears up on its own, but it can be treated by washing the bumps daily with an antibacterial soap for several weeks. If they persist, your child's doctor can remove the tops of the bumps with chemicals or abrasion, after which you should continue to use the antibacterial soap until healing is complete.

We have reached the end of this brief journey through the world of skin problems. Some of those you see will fall neatly into one or another of the categories we've discussed but most will not. If you cannot diagnose the problem, don't be chagrined. Your doctor may well wind up equally perplexed.

Lumps and Bumps

Sometimes, looking at their child's skin, parents discover an unusual bump beneath the surface. Most lumps and bumps are not very serious. If you have any question about them, have your doctor examine them to identify their origin and calm your fears.

Many bumps are normal bone contours, which can be more prominent on one side of the body than the other.

Large lumps can appear on the skull of newborn babies after a difficult delivery. These harmless swellings are collections of fluid or blood between the skin and the skull. They may take weeks to disappear, and often form a little crater before going away.

Older children's bumps are often simply bruises or little cysts. Cysts are pockets of fluid, about the size of a dime, directly under the skin, often on the eyelid or the back of the neck. Sometimes you can move them as though they were little marbles under the skin. Some are on joints such as the wrist, and move back and forth as the bones move; these are called ganglions. Most cysts do not require treatment, but it is best to point them out to the doctor.

Tumors are growths of tissue; happily, most of them are benign. Some are growths of blood or lymph vessels (hemangioma, lymphangioma); others are lumps of fat (lipoma) or of bone (osteoma). In short, this kind of lump may develop in just about any tissue. Your doctor will probably want to examine such lumps to see if they need to be removed.

A bump in the neck is often a lymph node. People sometimes call them "glands," but they are in fact small, rubbery, circular organs that help the body recognize and fight infection. Almost any infection can cause the lymph nodes to enlarge—they tend to swell during illness or when there is an inflammation nearby. Many viral infections cause enlargement; so do strep and mononucleosis. Lymph nodes are most often felt on cr near the neck and in the groin, and less commonly in the armpit, at the elbow, or behind the knee. It is common to find swollen lymph nodes in the groin of children who walk barefoot and get small splinters and cuts on their feet.

Enlarged lymph nodes are often as big as a large grape. They are usually slightly tender. If touching them hurts your child, especially if the overlying skin is red and warm, the nodes themselves may be infected, and antibiotics may be required. Most commonly, however, enlarged lymph nodes slowly shrink all by themselves, though it may take months or even years. And, just to drag things out a bit, the lymph nodes are likely to swell again to fight later infections.

When *do* we worry about lumps? They should certainly be examined if they are unusually hard and seem attached to underlying tissues, or if they are growing steadily (especially if larger than a walnut), or if there are other symptoms without a clear cause, such as fever, sweating, or weight loss.

It is reasonable to seek advice about any lump or bump that cannot be explained easily and persists for several days. The doctor may wish to see a child several times over a few weeks, just to be sure that a lump that looks harmless stays that way or goes away entirely.

Allergies

Does my child have allergies? We hear this question every day when parents call to tell us about the itchy, blotchy rash that suddenly appeared after their child ate strawberries, or the puffy, watery, itchy eyes after their little one petted a stray cat, or the wheezing after the youngster has been playing on a dry, grassy soccer field, or the runny nose that always plagues their child from April to August.

Signs of allergy range from the obvious to the very subtle. On the one hand, many symptoms are casually attributed to allergies without much basis. Although most allergic conditions can be treated at home by parents in consultation with their child's doctor, *if the child is having a very acute reaction involving difficulty in breathing or swelling of the mouth or throat, he should be seen by his doctor immediately.* Fortunately, such serious reactions are very rare.

Children can be allergic to virtually any substance. Common examples are foods such as milk and wheat, dyes and other food additives, drugs, insect venoms, pollens, grasses and weeds, cigarette smoke, dust, mold, animal dander, saliva or urine, various clothing materials, nickel pajama snaps, soaps, and chemicals. Allergic reactions can manifest themselves in a great variety of symptoms, depending on what part of the body is affected. They may include itchy, watery, bloodshot eyes; sneezing, runny nose; itchy throat; coughing; wheezing; eczema; hives (red, blotchy rash with white centers); diarrhea; vomiting; headache; crankiness; and fatigue. Since all of these symptoms are also seen in non-allergic conditions, the challenge to the doctor is to determine when they are actually the result of an allergic process. Swelling of the eyelid or lips, and hives, for example, are often due to viral illnesses.

Allergies certainly produce symptoms and discomfort, but they need not be thought of as illnesses. In fact, allergic reactions are simply an exaggeration of one of the body's protective defenses. The normal human immune system responds to foreign substances (antigens) that it perceives as harmful, by producing various proteins called antibodies, which are released into the bloodstream and tissues. Antibodies then play a role in the removal of these foreign substances. The immune system of the allergic child, however, reacts even to harmless substances by producing antibodies. (One of the antibodies, called IgE, can be measured in the blood as a general indicator of allergic tendency. Blood cells called eosinophils often increase in number when allergic reactions are taking place.) Something that to a nonallergic child is a nonthreatening antigen is an "allergen" to a child whose immune system is so sensitized. When the allergen and the antibodies meet at various places in the body, local reactions are set in motion by the release of histamine and other substances that result in the symptoms of allergy. The type of reactions and specific symptoms are determined by where the antibodies and allergen meet. When an irritating substance is inhaled and produces a reaction in the lungs, the result may be spasm of the small air tubes (bronchioles) causing wheezing, or asthma. A meeting in the nasal passages results in the release of histamine, the chemical mediator of allergic reactions, which causes watery eyes and a runny nose (hay fever). In the skin the allergen-antibody reaction causes itching, hives, or eczema. In the digestive tract the allergic reaction created by eating particular foods may cause nausea, abdominal cramps, or diarrhea. Swelling of the lips and eyelids can be part of a more generalized allergic reaction. Combinations of these symptoms may also occur.

Why do some children develop allergies and others not? Genetic, environmental, seasonal, and emotional factors determine who is allergic to what and when the allergic child will have symptoms. When both parents have a history of eczema, hay fever, or asthma themselves, it is very likely that their children will, at some time, show some signs of allergy. Other children will develop allergies even though there is no history of allergies in their family. Those children with a propensity to develop allergies may not exhibit any symptoms until they encounter certain specific foods, pollens, animals, or other allergens. Some children will not exhibit allergies until they have repeated exposure to multiple antigens. Symptoms in other allergic children can be triggered by infection, exercise, or emotional pressures.

Can allergies be prevented? The symptoms of allergy can be prevented if the allergens can be identified and avoided. Parents must become painstaking detectives. It often takes months to determine what triggers various allergic reactions.

In children who have inherited a tendency to allergies, the early introduction of cow's milk and solid foods may bring out reactions, because more substances can enter the bloodstream via intestinal absorption during early infancy. Recognizing that most babies' nutritional needs can be met by breast milk or formula for the first six months, we try to delay the introduction of solids as long as possible, especially those known to provoke allergic reactions. It is important to allow enough time between the introduction of one new food and the next, say four or five days, to observe the child for allergic reactions. Although yogurt may be tolerated by eight months, for example, we usually do not introduce cow's milk, citrus fruits and juices, or eggwhite until the baby is ten to twelve months old. Children with pronounced milk sensitivity may require soy formula instead of milk-based formula. Some babies can tolerate only very small amounts of foods to which they are sensitive. Breast milk, of course, is the least sensitizing food for infants.

When children have intestinal reactions or develop hives, we ask parents to carefully scrutinize what the child is eating. Any food can act as an allergen. Some of the chief offenders are cow's milk, nuts, eggs, chocolate, citrus, wheat and other grains, berries, and spices. Food colorings, preservatives, and medicines can also be allergens. If a particular food is suspect, we eliminate it from the diet for two to three weeks. Some pediatricians choose to eliminate only one food at a time, while others eliminate several foods at once and reintroduce them one at a time.

If we suspect that a child is allergic to something in his environment, we ask his parents to search the house for common allergens. Environmental allergens include house dust, cigarette smoke, feathers (birds, down pillows, comforters), fur (animals, rugs, clothing), wool (clothes, rugs), straw, horsehair (rug pads and furniture stuffing), mold, plants, pollens, and grasses. Pets are common culprits. Interestingly enough, the saliva and urine of dogs and cats, as well as the fur itself, are thought to be allergens. The cat licks its fur and the allergic child encounters the allergen when he pets the cat. Animals can leave their allergenic calling cards behind in a house even when they have moved away. We have occasionally been stumped when a family without pets moves into a house previously occupied by pets. The children wheeze and sneeze and, after an exhaustive search, we have the carpets cleaned and find the allergies resolved.

Seasonal allergies are a bit easier to pin down. Winter allergies often include mold and specific trees such as pines. Spring and summer allergies can be traced to several grasses, flowers, and pollens. Fall allergies are often caused by various pollens and dry leaves.

When the offending allergens cannot be identified in a child who is bothered by his symptoms, skin testing may be appropriate. This is done by placing tiny amounts of common allergens over small scratches on the arm and recording the skin reactions. Blood tests can measure IgE, eosinophil count, and antibody reactions to specific allergens.

Once the offending substances have been identified, the symptoms can be controlled by avoiding the allergens. We ask parents to dust frequently, to use a damp mop for cleaning floors, and to avoid vacuuming the child's room since this will spread the dust. We ask them to remove dust collectors such as books and stuffed animals from bedrooms or at least from around the bed. Wool spreads and feather-filled comforters are best put away and replaced by cotton and polyester blankets. Mattresses should be enclosed in zippered covers. Wall-to-wall carpet is to be avoided. Parents can use chlorine bleach or Lysol to eradicate mold. To minimize contact with pollen that may be blown in from the outside, an air conditioner, air filter, or ionizer can be used. Forced-air heating vents should be closed and sealed shut, even in the summer, to avoid circulating dust and pollen. Air and heater filters should be changed monthly. Families can rarely be persuaded to give up the family dog or cat—often the "first child" of the family. In such cases these animals should remain outside or at least not be allowed to sleep in an allergic child's room.

When parents must paint or use insecticides, an allergic child should not be present. Cigarette, pipe, and cigar smoke are other noxious irritants to be avoided. If you must smoke, do so outside.

When avoiding specific allergens is impossible, other treatment options can be explored. Some doctors will recommend desensitization which involves giving the child a series of injections containing small amounts of the allergen over a period of eighteen months or two years. Desensitization is a well-recognized treatment for children allergic to bees or other insect venom. The parents of such children should, in the meantime, always have on hand an emergency insect-sting kit that contains epinephrine (adrenalin) and an antihistamine.

Treatment of allergies depends on each child's particular symptoms. Antihistamine medications counteract the effects of histamine reactions. There are various kinds of antihistamines, some more useful for allergic coughs and nasal congestion, some for itching and swelling of the skin. Most antihistamines make children drowsy, which limits their use somewhat, but some newer preparations have fewer side effects. Another drug called cromolyn sodium inhibits the release of histamine by cells, but works best when taken preventively over a long period of time. Prescribed medications to dilate the bronchi are quite effective in treating asthma. They may be given as an injection, a syrup, a tablet, or they can be inhaled. Very young children can inhale bronchodilator medication through a mask or tubing using a machine at home, whereas older children may use a small portable inhaler. Corticosteroids may be prescribed when treating severe asthmatics or children with significant skin reactions. Allergic reactions that cause tightness in the throat or swelling of the eyes and face are usually treated with antihistamines but may also require adrenaline steroids.

There are some situations where anticipatory treatment can prevent wheezing. Children who wheeze only after vigorous exercise may benefit from an inhalation treatment before exercising. For those children who wheeze only when they have an infection, the doctor may prescribe a bronchodilator at the start of any respiratory illness.

Learning to live with allergies does not mean ignoring them, though. Irritability, tension, fatigue, and recurring headaches can accompany even relatively mild allergies and inhibit a child's level of functioning both at school and at home. Parents and doctor need to work together to give appropriate treatment without making the allergy the major focus of everyone's attention. An asthmatic or allergic child should not be considered frail or unable to participate in vigorous activities. With proper care, these children can, and should, have a fully active and fun-filled childhood.

Eye Problems

Whenever something happens that involves the eye, parents and doctors tend to be concerned. And rightly so! The eyes are a vital and delicate sense organ. The most common symptoms of several conditions are redness, itching, and pain. Irritation of the eye is common in children; the causes range from a clogged tear duct to allergy, chemical irritation, infection, or trauma of the eyelid and surrounding tissues. The extent of the problem and the accompanying symptoms determine whether the condition requires immediate attention.

In most healthy newborn infants, an overflow of tears or an accumulation of yellow material may be occasionally observed in the inner corner of the eyes. This condition, called lacrimal duct stenosis, is due to a narrowing of the duct that drains tears. Unless the drainage turns green or the whites of the eyes become red, this condition may be treated by massaging the corner of the eye, where it meets the nose, several times a day. Use your forefinger to apply pressure in a gentle circular motion.

Conjunctivitis, commonly known as "pinkeye," may occur at any age. The whites of the eyes become red due to an inflammation of the conjunctiva, one of the eye's coverings. Conjunctivitis is often accompanied by yellow or green drainage, swelling of the eyelid rims, itching, and sensitivity to light. Chemical conjunctivitis occurs as a reaction to an environmental irritant. Whenever any chemical, such as hair spray, enters a child's eye, it is best to wash the eye with water (not with boric acid) for at least fifteen minutes, using an eye cup or running tap water. Often this will meet with great resistance, but it is important to persevere. You should call your doctor or the nearest poison control center for further instructions as soon as possible. If exposure to smoke, smog, chlorine, or salt water has irritated the eyes to the point of requiring treatment, cool compresses and artificial-tear eye drops may be helpful until you can see your doctor.

Allergic conjunctivitis tends to be a seasonal occurrence

and is usually accompanied by sneezing, itching nose and palate, swollen eyelids, and watery discharge. Treatment consists of applying a cool compress to the eye, using medicated eye drops to constrict the blood vessels on the surface of the eye and reduce histamine release, or using oral antihistamines.

Viral conjunctivitis often accompanies a cold and is characterized by a thin, light-colored discharge, with some redness of the eye lining. It is highly contagious, and your child should be isolated from other children for several days until the discharge has disappeared. There is no specific treatment for viral conjunctivitis. To make your child more comfortable, wipe his eye gently with a cotton ball soaked in cool water several times a day. An eye clouded with discharge is most annoying; it could make anyone cranky. If there is eye pain or the conjunctivitis lasts more than seventy-two hours, the doctor should examine the child.

Bacterial conjunctivitis causes pus and a thick, yellow drainage with crusting of the lids and redness of the whites of the eyes. If left untreated, it may persist for weeks. The doctor will prescribe antibiotic drops or ointments, but if the eye fails to respond, the child should be reexamined to rule out ear or sinus involvement. Since bacterial conjunctivitis is easily spread to other children, your child should remain home from school until forty-eight hours after treatment has begun or until the discharge has stopped.

If the eyelid itself becomes swollen and discolored, the child may have a less common but more serious problem called periorbital cellulitis. This condition is sometimes accompanied by fever and listlessness and requires aggressive treatment to prevent the spread of infection to the eye itself. If your child looks like he has a black or purple eye, accompanied by swelling and discharge, he should be seen by a doctor as soon as possible.

If a foreign body has entered the eye, washing may be sufficient, or it may be necessary to remove the foreign body from the lid with a moistened cotton swab. This must be done with great caution! Turn the lid inside out over another cotton swab and hold its edge against the rim of the eye. Don't try this unless your doctor has shown you how to do it and you feel confident about your skill. Otherwise it is safer to have the doctor remove the foreign body. If trauma to the eye results in pain lasting longer than just a few minutes, patch the eye and call the doctor. Scratches of the cornea require attention; they may not be detectable except by eye examination. A common cause of corneal abrasion is the expressive swipe of a cat's paw.

A sty is not technically an eye problem. It resembles a pimple on the eyelid but is actually a collection of fluid in the hair follicle of an eyelash. The whites of the eyes are typically clear. A sty is nothing to worry about though it may persist for weeks before draining and disappearing. Sometimes a residual bump lasts for months. Home treatment consists of warm compresses applied several times a day. A course of antibiotics may be prescribed at some point. Sties can become infectious, so your child should use his own towel and keep his hands away from the infected eye. Another eyelid irritation is a flaky crusting called blepharitis. It may be treated initially with repeat applications of no-tears baby shampoo. Apply the shampoo twice a week and rinse off thoroughly.

Any child with persistent changes in vision, blurring, tearing, blinking, or squinting should be examined by his doctor. Eyes occasionally drift and cross in infants less than four months old. Crossing of the eyes in older children may be abnormal, and vision may be suppressed in one eye. This condition, called amblyopia, is best treated if detected early. The initial approach most often is to patch the "good" eye for some time and force the "lazy" eye to see. While most children are slightly farsighted, difficulty seeing close or far objects should be checked out. Persistent double vision or blurred vision could be due to a number of eye and neurological conditions and should be brought to the doctor's attention.

While many eye disorders are due to minor problems, it is safer to err on the side of early intervention. So don't be afraid to call your child's doctor if symptoms do not subside quickly.

Urinary-Tract Disorders

The urinary tract includes the kidneys, the ureters (tubes carrying urine from the kidneys to the bladder), the bladder, the urethra (the tube carrying urine from the bladder to the meatus), and the meatus (the opening through which we urinate).

When considering problems in the urinary tract, we most often begin by looking at the urine, which can give us valuable information about the health of the whole body as well as the health of the kidneys and the bladder.

First, we evaluate the color and the concentration of the urine. Urine is usually clear and yellow becoming darker when it is concentrated, and cloudy if bacteria or crystals are present. If urine is dark brown—especially if the child is feeling ill—it may be a sign of hepatitis. Reddish-brown urine may indicate bleeding somewhere in the urinary tract, and should be analyzed by the child's doctor. Keep in mind, however, that food dyes and medications can affect the color of urine; if your child has pink or brown urine, find out what he has eaten recently or what medications he is taking before you become alarmed. You may find orange crystals resembling face powder on your newborn baby's diaper. These are metabolites—a metabolic breakdown product—of uric acid. They are commonly found in the urine of infants. You may also find odd-colored stains on the diapers. These are probably only the results of urine reacting with various bleaches and chemicals used to clean diapers.

Next, we check to see if sugar or protein is present in the urine. Testing for sugar is a way to detect diabetes, and checking for protein is another way to evaluate the health of the kidneys. Some children have small amounts of protein in their urine, but it is usually of no significance. Elevated levels of ketones, another waste product, usually indicate that the child hasn't eaten for a few hours, but they can—rarely—signify disease, such as untreated diabetes.

A child's way of urinating can also be a clue to potential problems. The parents of one four-year-old boy noticed that he never urinated directly into the toilet. Although this is often due merely to a lack of attention, it could signal a fairly common condition known as hypospadias, in which the urethral meatus (opening of the urethra at the tip of the penis) is irregularly placed, making a straight stream of urine impossible. Hypospadias may be so slight as to go unnoticed except by Mom, but it may also cause quite irregular function and require surgical repair.

Both boys and girls may occasionally complain of a burning sensation when they urinate. This is often the result of urethritis, an inflammation or irritation of the urethra. It is commonly caused by bubble baths or shampoo irritating the urethra. It's best to avoid bubble baths entirely, and to delay soaping until the end of the bath, so that your child is not sitting in irritating soapy water for too long. Urethritis can also be caused by bacteria entering the urethera. This condition is often a problem with three- and four-year-old girls who insist on wiping themselves after bowel movements but wipe too vigorously or wipe in the wrong direction or not at all. Girls should be taught to wipe from front to back following urination and a bowel movement, to avoid contaminating the urethra. If your child's meatus looks red, you can treat it at home by giving sitz baths with plain warm water twice a day, followed by an application of zinc oxide or other soothing ointment. If the problem does not improve in two or three days, the child should be examined by her doctor. If she complains of itching, she could have yeast or another infection, which requires a doctor's attention.

Little boys may get sores on the tip of the penis from the ammonia in urine, the chemicals in soaps, or from the irritation of zippers or excessively vigorous maneuvers on bicycles. These can be treated at home with an antibiotic ointment. Bleeding, irritation, or infection of the foreskin of an uncircumcised boy may be the result of either too vigorous cleaning or neglect. If swelling occurs, cool compresses should be applied and the doctor should be notified; antibiotic treatment may be necessary. In caring for an uncircumcised boy it is important not to force the foreskin of the penis to retract. Free movement of the foreskin usually begins spontaneously when the child is two or three years old—perhaps with a little help from the average toddler, who is usually very interested in his penis. Once the foreskin is easily retractable, a boy can be taught to pull it back gently while bathing and to rinse with clear water. (See chapter on genital disorders.)

Infections of the urinary tract are not common in children, but they do occur. It is difficult to detect urinary infections in a very young infant. A urine analysis and culture may be done if an infant has an unexplained high or recurrent fever. This step is most important because urinary-tract infections in a very young child may be caused by a congenital anomaly of the urinary tract.

In toddlers any persisting change in urination patterns

should be investigated. An example would be the resumption of daytime wetting in a previously trained child. If a toddler cries when urinating and has a high fever with no other symptoms, a urinalysis and a urine culture should be done. If bacteria are present, the child will be treated with antibiotics, and a second culture will be taken a few weeks later. Some doctors like to check while the child is still on the medication to see if the infection is clearing properly. If a child has recurrent infections, the possibility of more serious urinary-tract problems can be ruled out with other tests, such as a sonogram (ultrasound) of the kidneys and x-rays of the urinary system. Depending on the nature of the child's urinary infection, associated symptoms, and the child's sex and general health, such an evaluation may be called for after several infections.

In older children we look for the more typical symptoms of painful frequent urination and urgency in getting to the toilet. These symptons call for a urine culture; if bacteria are growing in the urine, the youngster is usually treated with antibiotics.

When a child with a high fever complains of severe pain in the middle to low back, usually adjacent to the spine, kidney infection may be the cause. The symptoms of painful urination and urgency may or may not be present, but such a child should always be evaluated by a doctor. Hospitalization may be necessary if the infection does not respond to oral antibiotics.

It is not uncommon for children with a normal urinalysis and urine culture to complain of urinary frequency. Occasionally this is a symptom of pinworm infection. More commonly, it is the result of tension, and once that final exam or swim meet is over, the symptoms subside.

Tension is also a main cause of daytime "accidents." On the other hand, nighttime wetting, or enuresis, is so common that it is considered normal at least until age six. Often it runs in families. Enuretic children are characteristically heavy sleepers. A washable sleeping bag or two can free a child from having to wear diapers to bed. Some doctors advocate restricting fluids in the evening, voiding late at night, and (rarely) medication. Patience and understanding remain the best treatments.

Genital Disorders

"It's a boy!" "It's a girl!" These are usually the first words that ring out in the delivery room when a baby is born. Parents quickly check their newborn, typically counting fingers and toes and checking the genitals—which, happily, usually are normal. Of course, they are concerned if their baby's genitalia look different from the genitalia of other babies. In order to appreciate the range of differences in genital development and appearance, it is helpful to have an understanding of the formation and maturation of the genital tract.

During fetal development, the testes in boys and the ovaries in girls begin their growth in the abdominal cavity. During the last weeks of fetal life, the testes descend into the scrotum via the inguinal canal, and at the time of birth two testicles are usually found in the scrotum. A girl's ovaries, of course, remain in the abdominal cavity, and the canal of Nuck, which is similar to the inguinal canal, closes off. If either of these canals does not close completely, a part of the intestine may be displaced into it; this condition is a form of hernia. In girls, an ovary may slide down and appear as a swelling above the vulva. In boys, in whom hernias are more common than they are in girls, a swelling will be seen just above or within the scrotum. Most hernias are not painful.

However, if there is pain or discoloration beneath the skin, an ice pack should be placed on the swelling and the child's doctor should be called immediately. Often the ice will decrease the swelling and the hernia will be temporarily reduced. The definitive treatment for a hernia is a simple operation whereby the wandering intestine is returned to the abdominal cavity and the passageway is closed. This is not an illness but rather a weakness or variation in the normal course of development.

In addition to understanding fetal development, parents find it useful to have a sense of the timing and sequence of their child's subsequent development.

The Penis and the Testicles

Many parents comment on the size of their newborn son's scrotum, partly with pride and partly with concern. It is not unusual for the scrotum to appear quite large at birth, when fluid often accumulates around the testicles. This is called a hydrocele, and the fluid is usually reabsorbed by the body within the first year of life. Occasionally, this benign collection of fluid remains or reaccumulates later and may be associated with a hernia.

At the time of birth, the testicles have usually both descended into the scrotum. They look like small, round, smooth pebbles in the scrotal sac; they are not tender. One may be larger than the other and often one is set lower. Occasionally one or both of the testicles cannot be found in the scrotal sac at birth. The child's doctor will monitor the baby, and if the testicles have not descended by the time the child is around three years old he may suggest hormonal treatment (which is not always effective) or surgery. It is not uncommon for a baby boy to have a wandering testicle, one that lies in the scrotum most of the time but may move up out of the scrotum in reaction to cool air. It usually returns to the scrotum when the child takes a warm bath.

Very rarely a testicle may twist upon itself causing the child great pain and nausea. The testicle will appear blue and swollen. This is an emergency situation known as testicular torsion and should be immediately reported to the child's doctor.

Many parents agonize over the question of whether or not to circumcise their son. Circumcision is not necessary for medical reasons. While for some parents the decision is based on religious beliefs and is therefore an easy one, for others it is a social decision and more difficult. Some fathers want their sons to be circumcised because they themselves were. Others feel that it's unnecessary to perpetuate a ritual they do not feel strongly about. Many parents in the United States want their son circumcised because most boys in this country are and they don't want him to appear different. Periodically, there are articles written and claims made about an increase in the incidence of urinary tract infections in uncircumcised boys and men, but it is not clear whether this is significant or even true. If you decide to have your son circumcised, it should be done within the first few days or weeks of life. Occasionally, a pediatrician will postpone the procedure for several months if the child has a hypospadias (an unusually placed urethral opening). Following circumcision, the routine care of the penis involves washing it in the same way as the rest of the body. If the penis is left uncircumcised, no special care is required. Eventually the foreskin will separate from the glans (the tip of the penis). It may take five or more years to do so but there is no rush! No attempts should be made to force the foreskin to retract since this can cause pain, bleeding, and adhesions between the foreskin and the penis. After the foreskin retracts of its own accord, the child can be taught to gently pull the skin back and wash the glans underneath with plain water. The soft, white, cheese-like matter that frequently accumulates under the foreskin is not a sign of infection but merely superficial skin cells that have been sloughed off from the inside surface of the foreskin and the tip of the penis. These cells are continually shed throughout life and are no cause for concern.

Parents are often concerned about how they will care for their newborn's penis and are relieved to hear that the body generally cares for itself. However, occasionally parents may notice a rash or irritation of the penis or its adjacent skin. The glans or tip of the penis is normally a purplish color. Abrasion from a diaper or chemical irritation from urine may cause blistering or redness. The urethral meatus (opening for urine) may become red from diaper irritation, urine burn, or from a toddler pulling on his penis. Cool baths or compresses and soothing creams or ointments (Desitin, Caldesene, A and D Ointment) will make the child more comfortable and protect the area from further irritation.

Rashes that affect other areas of the body may also affect the penis. We commonly see heat and yeast rashes. Heat rashes clear up with a good airing. Yeast infections usually require treatment with a prescription medication or with a mixture of gentian violet and zinc oxide, an old-fashioned remedy that is messy but often effective. Small white pustules or oozing sores on the penis could be caused by a bacterial infection. The initial treatment for an infection consists of washing the area with an antibacterial soap, such as pHisoDerm, Betadine, or Hibiclens, and then applying an antibiotic cream like Bacitracin or Polysporin. If the infection does not begin to clear within a few days or if it spreads, your child should be seen by his doctor.

Discharges from the urethral meatus are rare and should be reported to the child's doctor. Warts and any unusual looking sores on the penis, at any age, should also be checked by a doctor to rule out the possibility of venereal disease. (We do not expect venereal disease unless we are dealing with a sexually active youngster or a child who has been sexually abused.)

The Female Genital Tract

Parents are often timid about caring for the external genitalia (the clitoris, vulva, and opening of the vagina) of their newborn daughter. The vulva may appear red and swollen, or there may be a white or bloody discharge from the vagina. These are normal phenomena and are not a cause for worry. While in utero, the baby's uterus is stimulated by her mother's hormones, and after birth, when these hormones are withdrawn, the infant's body may react with what is essentially a small menstrual period. Another consequence of these hormonal changes may be a vaginal adhesion. Occasionally a mother will notice a change in the appearance of the labia of her two- or three-month-old daughter. The labia, which were separated from one another at birth, may appear to be fused. This change is a result of decreasing estrogen in the baby's body. The labia will separate again as the little girl develops. If the area becomes irritated or if the child has recurrent urinary tract infections, however, estrogen cream may be applied to the labial skin to cause the adhesions to disappear. This treatment often needs to be repeated two or three times to be effective.

It is not uncommon for little girls to have a clear or slightly cloudy vaginal discharge throughout childhood. This discharge may increase or become thicker as the child approaches puberty. If the discharge becomes blood-streaked or discolored, it should be reported to the doctor. Just as a child may place small objects in her ears or nostrils, so she may also place a bead or small object in her vagina; this can cause a foul-smelling, discolored discharge. Yeast infections are a common cause of vaginal discharge, especially in older girls. A yeast infection may follow treatment with antibiotics or it may be the result of running around on a hot day in a damp bathing suit, which creates a perfect environment for the yeast organism. This discharge usually resembles white curdled cheese and is rather itchy. Mild infections can be treated with sitz baths of cool water to which a cup of white vinegar has been added. If baths are not effective, your child's doctor may prescribe an antifungal cream such as ny-tatin or Lotrimin.

Pinworm infections are another cause of vaginal discharge and itching (see chapter on infections). Infections such as gonorrhea, gardnerella, or trichomonas can also cause vaginal discharge. It is most uncommon in younger girls but should be considered when a foul-smelling, discolored discharge persists. Your child's doctor may culture the discharge to see if such an infection is present.

Other types of irritation may affect the vulva and the female urethra. Bubble bath is a common source of urethral and vaginal irritation and should be avoided. Skin irritation can also be caused by detergents and softeners used to wash underwear.

To avoid the possibility of irritation or infection, it is important to teach little girls to wipe themselves after urinating and after bowel movements by patting the urethra and by wiping from the front to the back.

Most girls have little awareness of their internal genital organs. Occasionally, the ovaries can be the cause of abdominal pain. Some girls may feel mild abdominal pain in the middle of their menstrual cycle. This is called "mittelschmerz" and is of no significance. It is not unusual for an ovary to enlarge slightly or for a small cyst to grow on an ovary, and occasionally a youngster may be aware of this. Severe, unrelenting pain may be caused by a twisting of the ovary. Infection of the uterus or the fallopian tubes may also cause abdominal pain, fever, and a foul-smelling vaginal discharge. Any of these conditions should be evaluated by your daughter's doctor.

Most children have very healthy, normal-appearing genitalia and are not bothered by much other than some of the nuisances we have discussed.

As your children begin to grow up and become interested in their bodies and their development, you will discover a new challenge, that of comfortably observing your children's growth and anticipating the many questions children ask and don't ask about changes they observe in their bodies. Some parents find it very easy and natural to talk with their children about their genitals while others are not sure what terms to use or when to update what they think their children already know. It is important to feel comfortable with the terms you use and to give pertinent, age-appropriate, information that neither overwhelms a child nor fails to satisfy him or her.

When two-year-olds start to talk, we teach them the names of the various parts of their body and show delight as they respond with the proper words for nose, hand, eyes, toes. It is important to include the names of the genitals as well so that children can be comfortable with their entire body and so that we can talk about the genitals as we teach our children to care for themselves. During the preschool years, when we hope to be instilling good health habits, we must deal with issues of bathing and wiping after bowel movements. We also teach our children not to handle their genitals too roughly and not to put objects into the penis or the vagina. With the current awareness of child abuse, we certainly want our children to be able to tell us if they have been treated inappropriately. To do so, they need some vocabulary, and some indication that parents are comfortable with their own bodies as well as with their children's bodies.

Many families use terms such as "private parts" to convey the idea that the genital area is special—and private. You may be tempted to give cute names to the genitals. We think it is best to give children the correct words so they can communicate effectively in the real world. Certainly little boys are aware of their penis long before they have a name for it and are comfortable with the words penis and testicles (testes) when they start to use language. Little girls will have a hard time naming parts they cannot see such as ovaries, uterus, or vagina. However, vulva, labia, and clitoris are meaningful terms for the parts of their body they *can* see and feel. As preschoolers begin to encounter pregnant teachers and parents and start to have siblings, they will ask where the baby came from, where it is growing, and how it will get out of its mother's body. This is a logical time to introduce the terms ovaries, uterus, vagina, and sperm. Most children are pleased with exact names and simple explicit descriptions.

Young girls are very aware of their mother's body and may have some idea of menstruation long before adults begin to discuss it with them. As their friends' bodies begin to develop, children will have more questions and may be ready to talk about the changes that are about to occur in their own bodies. Between the ages of eight and twelve their annual physical examination is a good time for a child's doctor to discuss development and complement the discussions that you have at home. There are some lovely books available for prepubescent girls and boys to read with their friends and their families or in the privacy of their own rooms.

Children of both sexes will be relieved to hear that the age at which secondary sexual characteristics begin to appear (pubescence) differs for girls and boys; girls start to mature two to four years earlier than boys. Between the ages of eight and ten many youngsters appear a bit heavier than in previous years. Girls usually begin to assume their rounded female contours at about eight or ten. Breast development also begins during these years though a girl's breasts may not actually reach their full size until she is sixteen to eighteen years old. Between the ages of nine and thirteen, young girls may first notice pubic hair, which is initially straight, light, and scant, but eventually curly, darker, and more abundant. Hair is usually noticed under the arms shortly before the onset of menstruation, which may normally occur anytime between the ages of nine and sixteen.

During the year before the onset of menses, many girls notice that the slight vaginal discharge they have come to regard as just part of being a girl becomes a bit heavier and cloudy. They are very aware of a growth spurt which often has them towering over boys their age. These developmental milestones seem to be occuring earlier than they used to. In the United States the average age for beginning menstruation is twelve and a half, a year earlier than it was sixty years ago. Though some girls begin their periods as early as eight or as late as eighteen, it is advisable to check with your daughter's doctor if the onset of menses seems especially early or especially late. The period itself is often quite irregular for the first two to three years, both in its frequency and in the amount of menstrual flow. Knowing this is reassuring to both parents and the girls themselves. Occasionally, periods may become very heavy or increase in frequency. This change is usually associated with the hormonal ups and downs of early adolescence and is usually perfectly normal. Occasionally, heavy or frequent periods may have other causes, so it is wise to bring the matter to your doctor's attention.

Girls may worry about whether they will be plagued by

menstrual cramps. Though we hear a great deal about cramps, they are not a big problem for most girls. When they are, it is best to keep up a regular amount of activity and use mild pain relievers such as aspirin or acetaminophen, or some of the many new medications (such as ibuprofen, Advil) which may be taken right at the start of the period before cramps begin.

Boys generally begin to develop secondary sexual characteristics about two to four years later than girls, between ten and fourteen years of age. The earliest changes are usually an increase in the size of the scrotum and the testes at age ten to twelve, followed by a gradual increase in the size of the penis between ages eleven and fifteen. Many boys notice a swelling behind their nipples, which may be tender and is often only on one side of the chest. Such swelling may persist for several months and then disappear spontaneously. Voice changes occur at this time, and within a year of these changes most boys experience "wet dreams," or nocturnal emissions. Pubic and axillary hair appear as the testes and penis begin to enlarge. Such hair is initially very light but becomes darker, curlier, and more abundant over the next three or four years. Most boys first notice very light facial hair between fifteen and seventeen years of age. The period of the most rapid growth for boys is less predictable than for girls. It is usually two to three years after the onset of pubescent changes. Sperm maturation is also variable; relative infertility may extend to age fifteen to seventeen—but don't count on it.

Adolescents as well as younger children vary in their ability to express pleasure or concern about their growing, changing bodies. Your knowledge, sympathy, and understanding will help your child cope with growing up.

Accidents

*H*ow did it happen? How did it happen so *fast*? Parents ask themselves these questions when their child has an accident, but the very nature of accidents is that they do happen, often for reasons we can never pin down. Of course, you will do your best to disasterproof your home, but do not despair if some mishaps occur in spite of your best efforts. Being informed and prepared to help your child after an accident will make both of you feel calmer and may go a long way toward preventing serious consequences.

Injuries

When your child is injured, decisive action on your part is extremely important. Children naturally protect an injury;

they often cry and do not want to be touched. It is normal to be upset when we first see our child hurt or bleeding, and even to feel guilty about an injury if we were responsible for the child at the moment he was hurt, but we should not let the child's resistance or our own feelings interfere with our giving proper attention to the injury.

It is good for parents to be calm, soft-spoken, and re-assuring in the face of an injury, but by all means do whatever you must to find out what has happened and to begin appropriate treatment. The extent or consequences of an injury can often be minimized if treatment is given without delay.

Bruises

Blows cause black-and-blue bruises of varying sizes and hues depending on what part of the body was hit and how hard. For example, relatively mild bumps on the forehead may cause large goose eggs because many large veins run just beneath the skin there. Active children often get very colorful bruises on their shins. In other locations frequent bruises may be due to excessively rough play, but they may also signify that your child is easily bruised. If bruises occur in locations not easily explained by commonplace injuries, the doctor should be consulted. A heightened bleeding tendency could reflect a blood clotting problem. An unusual bruise, such as one on the back, might suggest nonaccidental trauma.

Bruises can be treated with ice or cool compresses. As the blood is gradually absorbed, a bruise will turn yellow and then fade.

Cuts and Scrapes

Scrapes are best treated by washing them with soap and water (or with hydrogen peroxide) and then applying an antibiotic ointment. To stop the bleeding of a cut, clean it, elevate the injured limb above the level of the heart, if possible, and apply ten minutes of steady pressure without interruption. If the cut is on the face, or if the bleeding does not stop, or if the wound is gaping, or completely through the lip, stitches may be required; call your doctor for instructions.

Cuts on the tongue and gums bleed a great deal for several minutes but usually heal without any intervention. Cool drinks will help stop the bleeding and prevent its recurrence.

If a tooth is knocked out of its socket, wash it and put it back, holding it gently in place while you call your dentist. If this is not possible, place it in cool water and contact your dentist immediately. If a tooth is chipped, the dentist should also be called, especially if a large portion of the tooth has been lost. Injured teeth may turn gray days after the accident, indicating possible root damage, or bleeding into the tooth. Your child should be examined by his dentist if this happens. You should also watch for pain or redness at the gumline, which could indicate infection.

Foreign Bodies

Foreign bodies are objects that find their way to places where they don't belong.

Children get many splinters by walking barefoot on wooden floors or during their first attempts at carpentry. Your approach to the splinters will depend on their size, number, location on the body, and source. For example, multiple hairlike redwood splinters on the sole of the foot, or fine cactus needles in the palm of the hand, should usually be cleaned thoroughly and then left alone. With continued washing, they usually work themselves out over a couple of weeks and do not become infected. Larger splinters can be removed after cleaning if they can be grasped with tweezers and pulled out without breaking. Some metal objects can be lifted off skin surfaces using a strong magnet. If a foreign body is left in the skin, a small amount of redness around the area is to be expected after several days, but if the area of redness is extending, if streaks of red are seen projecting from it, or if there is a yellow discoloration or discharge, infection could be setting in and the doctor should be called.

Other foreign bodies, such as beads or coins, can also find their way into the ears, nose, or throat. Most of these will have to be removed by the doctor unless the child himself takes care of the problem by sneezing or coughing the object out.

If the object has been "swallowed," you must learn to distinguish whether it has lodged in the trachea (windpipe, where it can interfere with breathing), or the esophagus (where it can interfere with swallowing) or has passed into the stomach. If the child is speaking or crying, not coughing, and not blue, the breathing passages are probably not affected. *If he is not breathing, or if he is coughing and turning blue, he requires prompt treatment using the principles of CPR directed against choking;* see the Appendix. Objects which lodge in the esophagus usually produce drooling and an inability to swallow. The child may actually point at his throat. If so, call your doctor; it may be necessary to remove the object (often a coin) using a tube. If the object has passed into the stomach, it may not be necessary to do anything, but the doctor should nevertheless be informed. The small, round, flat batteries that power cameras and so many other devices these days often contain toxic substances that may be released after being swallowed. If you suspect one of these has disappeared inside your child's mouth, call his doctor.

Another common target of foreign bodies is the eye. Usually the best approach is to rinse the eye for twenty minutes under running lukewarm tap water. An eye cup or syringe can also work well. The key to the success of this method is convincing your child to hold his eyelids open during the rinsing! If pain and redness are not diminishing after twenty minutes of rinsing, it is time to call the pediatrician, who will probably wish to examine the eye. If the foreign body is metallic, the emergency requires prompt examination. Children who wear contact lenses need to know that these too can behave like foreign bodies and may need to be removed. The rule of thumb for any eye injury is to call the physician if simple first aid measures do not work. A patch over the eye can help diminish movement and further irritation of the eye while getting to a doctor.

Toxic liquids aren't exactly foreign bodies, but if the skin is exposed to a dangerous substance (insecticide, for example), you should act as if they are. Remove all clothing and wash the skin thoroughly with soap and water.

Nosebleeds

Nosebleeds are often the result of a minor trauma or an exploring finger, but they can also happen spontaneously since the blood supply in the nose is rich and the mucus membranes are fragile. In most cases, mild pressure controls nosebleeds if applied long enough. Have the child sit with his head up or bend slightly forward and pinch the nostrils shut tightly for ten minutes (by the clock!). It is important not to peek! Having the child lie down or applying ice to the fore-head or nape of the neck are both ineffective. After ten minutes look into the throat to see whether blood is trickling down from the back of the nose. If the nosebleed continues despite two attempts to stop it, call your doctor. To prevent recurrent nosebleeds, you might try humidifying the child's room, turning down the heat, putting petroleum jelly into the child's nostrils morning and evening, and keeping little fingernails cut short.

Fainting

If your child faints, observe him closely. Nothing need be done if he is breathing and the airway is clear. Smelling salts and other noxious stimuli are not necessary; a child should regain consciousness without their help. If he fails to regain consciousness within two minutes, call for help. If you are away from a phone, carry the child with you when you go to call for help; do not leave him unattended.

Falls

Even though you may have been extremely careful about childproofing your home, even though you never leave your child unattended on the changing table, in an elevated infant seat, or on the bed, falls nevertheless are almost inevitable and begin as soon as your child begins to move. Happily, that awful sound of a child hitting the floor does not always mean serious injury.

If your child has an accidental fall, try not to let panic or guilt prevent you from giving him a calm, quick, top-to-bottom looking over to assess the extent of his injuries.

When a child bounces up, crying and screaming about a hurt arm, that may be the only injury, but be aware that other signs of injury elsewhere may appear later.

If you suspect a possible neck or back injury, do not move the child until these areas have been properly braced. In the event of a head injury, note unconsciousness, twitching movements, and the location of lumps or bruises, and report this information to the child's doctor at once. Additional signs of possible trouble include persistent clear fluid draining from the nose or an ear, which could be spinal fluid leaking through a broken skull bone; or the inability to move an arm or a leg, which could indicate an injury to brain tissue. Also watch for drowsiness, vomiting, and blurred vision—all signs of concussion.

Most doctors will treat a mild head injury or even a minimal concussion at home. Parents may be asked to shine a flashlight into the child's eyes once an hour for four hours and again after six to eight hours, watching to see that both pupils contract equally. If the child falls asleep, check at three to four hour intervals to be sure he can be roused, at least to the point of moving and uttering some purposeful sounds, and again test the pupil responses. Note any changes in mobility, speech, or thought patterns, and contact the child's doctor at once if any of these responses are abnormal or if a headache or vomiting persist beyond eight to ten hours. It is also important to contact the doctor if signs of concussion appear later, or if peculiar thought and behavior patterns are noted several days—or even weeks—after the injury.

Sprains and Fractures

The inability to move a limb usually signifies a sprain, dislocation, or fracture. Elevating the injured limb on a pillow and applying ice packs are appropriate first steps in treating such injuries. Even if it is a fracture, don't panic. Emergency casting usually is not required unless the bone is visibly out of alignment. Your doctor will advise how to move the child with the least pain and risk of further injury.

Some children see a cast as a mark of distinction and valor, testifying to their athletic prowess or bravery, a beautiful white surface just waiting for written messages of admiration and endearment. But casts are not always as much fun as they seem at first. Soon after being applied, they become hot and tight. If the skin below the margin of the cast is cold and swollen, the cast may be too tight. Some casts are left on for six weeks, and they can get old pretty fast! Though they should be kept dry and clean, it is often very hard to do. After a cast is removed, the limb may be stiff and require a period of exercise and physical therapy to restore full motion.

An injury particular to toddlers is a pulled or "dislocated" elbow. The "dislocation" actually is due to a piece of ligament that becomes caught between two pieces of bone. It characteristically leads to a dropped arm and wrist that hurts if a parent tries to manipulate it. Once the possibility of fracture has been ruled out, a pulled elbow may be realigned using a maneuver in which you grasp the child's hand as in a handshake and twist it palm downward while pulling gently and holding the elbow steady with your free hand. If the maneuver is successful a click is felt and the child is again able to use the arm. Usually your doctor would perform the maneuver, but he may ask you to try first. Don't try it without your doctor's go-ahead.

Sprains can be just as serious as fractures and are often as painful. When a joint such as an elbow, wrist, knee, or ankle is suddenly twisted, the ligament surrounding the joint may be stretched or torn, which produces bleeding and swelling. Minor sprains can be treated at home with rest, ice packs, wrapping, and elevation. If the sprain is more serious, it may require a long-term splint or even a cast. If the accompanying pain or swelling is severe, you should contact your doctor.

Burns

Despite our efforts to be careful, accidents do happen and the chance of a child getting burned or scalded is unfortunately still great. Wall and floor heaters, electrical appliances of all kinds, pans containing hot oil or food, barbecues, and smoldering fireplaces are only some of the hazards children are exposed to every day.

A fresh burn can look so frightening that parents may panic and fail to take appropriate first-aid measures. It is essential to act quickly, however, because a burn requires immediate attention to prevent extension of the injury to deeper layers of the skin.

If your child gets burned, apply cool compresses for three to five minutes.

After removing clothing and treating the burn with ice, examine it carefully. Any burn that blisters, breaks the skin, or turns white should be reported to the doctor, as should any burn or scald on the face.

Burns that cause redness only are generally first degree burns and heal without scarring. These burns require no further treatment after the initial cooling.

Burns that blister are usually second degree, which means they have penetrated through the first layer of skin. A formed blister should be left intact as long as possible to protect the area against infection. Should the blister break, tell the doctor. The burn may take two weeks to heal, but parents should be prepared for some temporary skin changes that may persist for several months. Initially the skin will be red and sensitive. It may burn more readily in the sun, so sunscreen is important. Eventually the skin will return to its normal color and texture but some slight differences may be permanent. Occasionally a scar may result from a deep second-degree burn. It may be minor or quite disfiguring, depending on the seriousness of the burn and also on its location and size. A plastic surgeon should evaluate a disfiguring scar.

Third-degree burns generally look white because all the layers of the skin have been injured. In third-degree burns there is also a loss of feeling in the burned area because nerves have been destroyed; consequently a serious burn may be less painful than a minor one. Because they scar when they heal, third-degree burns may eventually require skin grafts.

Whatever its degree, a burn over a joint may be more serious than one in another location since scarring may affect joint mobility. Substantial burns over joints should be examined by a doctor and may eventually require physical therapy and a plastic surgeon's evaluation.

When dressing a first-degree burn, aloe vera lotion or zinc oxide may be applied. Other preparations may be prescribed by your doctor for more severe burns. When you apply a dressing, be sure it does not stick to the skin surface. The primary purpose of a dressing is to protect the wound from dirt and further injury; aluminum foil is perfect in an emergency situation. Bulky nonstick gauze or a Kerlix bandage are also fine.

After the child has been treated, preventive measures and renewed vigilance are in order. A full discussion of how you can prevent accidents is contained in the chapter on home safety.

Electrical burns deserve some special discussion. Static electricity, the kind generated by walking across a carpet and discharged by touching a metal doorknob, causes a big surprise jolt but little damage. Telephone wire is usually not harmful, but exposure just when the phone is ringing can give a child contact with line current. Sockets, extension cords, and the like can cause significant shock and burns, especially in a toddler's mouth. *Disconnect the source of electricity* before touching the child. The most important step is to separate the child from the source of current without making contact with the electricity yourself. Next, you should call your child's doctor promptly. High voltage exposures, such as power lines, can be extremely serious and should be approached as major injuries. Power-line contacts, for example, may cause heartbeat irregularities in addition to burns and may require the initiation of cardiopulmonary resuscitation (CPR) once the victim is clear of the current.

Fortunately, most burns look worse than they are. The first and main point to remember is that treatment given in the first twenty minutes can do much to minimize the effect of a burn. The most important part of that treatment is *cool it down*.

Bites and Stings

Insect bites are as annoying to children as they are to adults —and usually of no greater importance! They itch, the child (or adult) scratches, and eventually the bites get better. The biggest problem is that scratching can cause a secondary skin infection.

Local reactions to bites can be impressive without being dangerous. The swelling often resembles a welt and can be an inch or more in diameter, but it does not mean that anything is seriously wrong or that your child is having an allergic reaction. Also, any insect bite on or near the eyelid can cause substantial swelling, but the eye itself is not affected and usually does not become inflamed. Most of the time, itching and swelling from an insect bite can be treated with cool compresses and a soothing cream such as aloe vera or with calamine lotion. Minor allergic rashes can also occur in response to insect bites. These can be confusing because they appear to be a second, unrelated rash. Most respond well to antihistamine medications.

Spider bites can produce large nickel- or quarter-size circular sores. A small central bite mark may be visible. The bites usually heal over a two-week period without special treatment. Black widows and spiders with a violin-shaped mark can cause more serious trouble. Call your doctor if you have captured such a culprit.

Scorpion bites can be dangerous, especially for younger children, and should be evaluated at a medical facility promptly.

How can insect and spider bites be prevented? We are asked these questions often, because bites are so annoying and ugly, and because the little creatures who inflict them have such reputations for spreading diseases. While it is true that insects—most often mosquitos and fleas—can spread certain diseases, most of these diseases are not prevalent in the United States. When a disease that can be transmitted by insect bites (encephalitis, for example, an inflammation of the brain) is known to be present in an area, public-health officials usually issue warnings alerting the community.

As far as general measures are concerned, using screens and nets is the best way to keep flying insects out of the house. Since insect repellants contain fairly potent chemicals, they should be used sparingly. It is better to cover as much of the body as possible with clothes and dot the exposed areas with repellant when necessary. Taking vitamin B_1 daily appears to render some people unappealing to insects. It might be worth a try!

Fleas can be controlled by treating pets that harbor them with periodic repellant dips and by fitting them with flea collars. New electronic flea collars contain no toxic chemicals whatsoever, and they may be effective. We are not enthusiastic, however, about flea bombs. They leave significant insecticide residues that could be toxic to children.

Stings are a somewhat different proposition. In the case of a bee or wasp sting, it is important to remove the stinger from the wound with a fingernail or card dragged firmly against the skin. Remember not to squeeze the stinger with tweezers, which may force more venom into the skin. If the local reaction is very large, an oral antihistamine such as Benadryl may be given.

A massive allergic reaction to a sting, in which a child has trouble breathing or loses consciousness, is very rare, but could require the initiation of CPR and emergency medical assistance. Your doctor should instruct you in the use of adrenalin injections if you know that your child is allergic to bee stings.

After a walk in the woods or through high grass, it is a good idea to check yourself and your child for ticks. They are tricky to remove, and it's important that it be done properly. Place tweezers around the tick as close to the skin as possible, then slowly and steadily pull it off the skin. If the body separates from the head, a small black dot will remain beneath the skin and may have to be removed by your doctor. If you're not sure you got the head, bring along the mortal remains of the removed tick for inspection.

Nonpoisonous snake bites should be treated as puncture wounds. This means careful washing and administration of a tetanus toxoid booster if your child's immunity has lapsed (boosters are advised every ten years for everyone over the age of five). If the snake is thought to be poisonous, avoid moving the affected limb. Do not apply ice or cut into the puncture. Suction may be beneficial, and commercial venom extractors, which look much like syringes, are available at camping supply stores. A constricting band, made with a strap or a shoelace, may be applied above a snake bite on an arm or leg to slow the advance of the poison. Such a band should not be applied to fingers or toes, and it should not be very tight—you should be able to slip a finger underneath it. The prolonged use of a tourniquet may constrict blood flow and has its own risks, so it is most important to get the child to a medical facility where antivenin can be given as soon as possible.

In the event of an animal bite, try to identify or capture the animal, if possible, so that the risk of rabies transmission can be evaluated. Wash the wound carefully with soap and water for fifteen minutes and call your doctor for instructions. Remember, most animal bites are from healthy, usually docile, pets that have been provoked. The bacterial infections that are likely to occur are easily treated; your doctor may decide to use preventive antibiotics, depending on the extent and location of the injury. A tetanus booster may also be recommended.

Nonetheless, animal bites can be bad enough to terrify child and parent alike. Sometimes wounds are large enough to require stitches to close them. Just remember, most animal bites are not serious, just scary.

Human bites are another proposition. Our mouths tend to harbor nastier bacteria than the mouths of family pets. Fortunately most human bites, those from toddler to toddler, tend to be quite superficial and cause more emotional than physical trauma.

Poisoning

Even though they often refuse those beautifully prepared vegetables we try to convince them to eat, most children under five years old will be tempted to eat or drink anything they discover as they journey through the house. About 300,000 children a year swallow poisonous materials; half of them are seriously injured, and at least three hundred die. It is not surprising that ninety percent of these healthy, curious children are under age five. It is a surprise that about ninety-five percent of them are under adult supervision when they so quietly find and swallow those dangerous materials we thought were hidden from them. The most commonly ingested poisons are medicines: aspirin, acetaminophen, vitamins, iron tablets, tranquilizers, stimulants, and hormones (thyroid extract and birth control pills). Other substances frequently swallowed are soaps, detergents and cleansers, disinfectants, insecticides, bleaches, glues, acids and alkalies (lye), floor and furniture polish and wax, cosmetics, and plant material, especially cigarette tobacco.

Poisonous substances can also be inhaled (carbon monoxide and gasoline fumes) as well as absorbed through the skin (certain insecticides), but most children are poisoned by substances they eat.

Most poisonings can be prevented. Poisonproof your house while your child is still an infant. Continuously reevaluate his ability to climb new heights, open new doors, and meet new challenges to his curiosity. Limit the number of medications and toxic household materials you accumulate. Since prescription drugs and over-the-counter preparations are the substances children most commonly ingest, take particular care to keep *all* medications, even the vitamin pills that frequently grace the breakfast table, locked away in a safe place out of sight. Don't rely on safety catches when dealing with poisonous materials. Be aware that the potential for poisoning and accidents is greatest during those times when the family is under stress, such as when a child is ill or at dinner time when everyone is rushing about. And be suspicious not only of new toys and plants but also of familiar materials such as the contents of a friend's purse. Be especially careful when visiting the homes of grandparents and friends who do not have young children—elderly people often get drugs in containers without childproof caps. Always supervise your child when you are shopping; stores and supermarkets display drugs conveniently within the reach of even the smallest child.

There are some other steps you can take to prevent disaster. Be aware of the medications you do have in the house. Make sure they are properly labeled and that they are currently effective (check the date of expiration on all prescription medicines). Discard outdated drugs by flushing them down the drain; don't discard them where children can find them. Don't take medicine in front of young children; they are mimics and may try to imitate you later. Though it is laborious, each time you take a medication record the number of tablets left in the container or draw a line at the level of liquid remaining in the bottle. Such information is most helpful if you ever need to estimate the amount of a medication your child has ingested. Don't buy large amounts of a drug. Though buying in bulk is more economical, the emotional and monetary cost following an accidental ingestion can be enormous. Get bottles with childproof caps, but don't rely on them.

When you give your child medicine, don't refer to it as candy; and don't allow a young child to give himself medicine. Always read the label and never give medicine in the dark. It is best to remove what you need and immediately put the bottle back in a secure place. A common five a.m. phone call to doctors is from a mother or father who, having given a sick child the appropriate amount of aspirin or acetaminophen during the night, wakes the next morning to find the child still asleep, the medicine bottle clutched in his little hand.

Household products are the second most commonly ingested poisons. Keeping them out of reach can be tedious, since the containers are often large and bulky, and you probably use them frequently. But it's well worth the effort! We advise parents to designate one high kitchen cabinet for household products and to install a padlock or an unobtrusive key lock on that cabinet. Be aware of the toxicity of the products you use (see Tables 2 and 3) and while your children are young, avoid keeping very toxic substances around the house. Read labels, which often include warnings; ask your pediatrician or the poison control center in your area to explain any terms you may not understand and to advise you on what to do if your child should swallow these substances. Always keep products in their original containers. Put on a clear, new label if the container becomes smudged. As with medications, always record the amount of liquid or powder left in the bottle or box after each use by drawing a line at the remaining level. Do not keep household products near food. Once again, don't rely on safety catches. They may slow a child down, but they won't stop the very determined toddler from finding treasures stored under the sink.

Some household products may become hazards after they are used. For example, care must be taken in choosing paints. Though few lead-based paints remain on the market, if you have moved into an old house be sure to check the lead content of the old paint before stripping or remodeling. Watch out, also, for old lead water pipes. Samples can be

TABLE 2
Toxic Products That Require
Treatment If Swallowed

If your child swallows any of these products, call your doctor or a
poison-control center immediately.

Acetaminophen
Acetone
After-shave lotion
Alcohol (isopropyl, less
    than 5 ml)
Ammonia
Amphetamine
Antifreeze
Arsenic
Aspirin
Battery acid
Benzene
Bichloride of mercury
Bleach (more than 5%
    sodium hypochlorite)
Boric acid
Brush cleaner
Camphor
Carbon tetrachloride
Charcoal-lighting fluid
Chlordane
Cologne
Cosmetics
DDT
Deodorant (some)
Detergent (less than 20%
    concentration)
Dishwasher granules
Drain cleaner
Fabric softeners
Floor polish
Fluoride

Furniture polish
Gasoline
Grease remover
Gun cleaner
Hair dye (some products
    toxic)
Hair preparations (some
    products toxic)
Hydrogen peroxide
    (stronger than 8% con-
    centration)
Indelible markers (some)
Ink
Insecticides
Iodine
Iron tablets
Kerosene
Lacquer thinner
Lye
Liniment
Medication, capsules
Medication, tablets
Medication, oral liquids,
    nonoily
Metal cleaner
Mothballs or cakes
Nail polish
Nail-polish remover
Naphtha
Narcotics
Oven cleaner
Paint (lead)

Toxic Products That Require Treatment If Swallowed (continued)

Paint thinner
Perfume
Permanent-wave
  neutralizer
Pesticides
Quicklime
Rat poison
Shoe polish
Strychnine
Suntan preparations

Toilet-bowl cleaner
Turpentine
Typewriter cleaner
Wart remover
Washing soda
Wax (floor or furniture)
Weed killer
Wick deodorizer
Wood preservative
Zinc compounds

TABLE 3
Products That Are Usually Nontoxic

Abrasives
Adhesives (small amount)
Antacids
Antibiotics
Baby-product cosmetics
Ballpoint-pen inks
Bathtub floating toys
Bath oil (castor oil and per-
  fume)
Bleach (less than 5% sodium
  hypochlorite)
Body conditioners
Bubble-bath soaps (deter-
  gents)
Calamine lotion
Candles (beeswax or paraf-
  fin)
Caps (toy pistols, potassium
  chlorate)
Chalk (calcium carbonate)
Clay (modeling)

Contraceptives
Corticosteroids
Cosmetics
Crayons (marked A.P., C.P.)
Dehumidifying packets (silica
  or charcoal)
Detergents (phosphate only)
Deodorants
Deodorizers (spray and re-
  frigerator)
Elmer's Glue
Etch-A-Sketch
Eye makeup
Fabric softeners
Fertilizers (if no insecticide or
  herbicides added)
Fish bowl additives
Glues and pastes
Golfball (core may cause
  mechanical injury)
Grease

Products That Are Usually Nontoxic (continued)

Hair products (dyes may be
   caustic; sprays, tonics)
Hand lotions and creams
Hydrogen perioxide (medici-
   nal 3%)
Incense
Indelible markers
Ink (black, blue—nonperma-
   nent)
Idophil disinfectant
Laxatives
Lipstick
Lubricant
Lubricating oils (lipoid pneu-
   monia)
Lysol disinfectant (not toilet-
   bowl cleaner)
Magic markers
Makeup (eye, liquid facial)
Matches (less then 20 wood
   or 2 books of paper)
Mineral oil (unless aspirated)
Newspaper (but chronic eat-
   ing may result in lead poi-
   soning)
Paint, indoor latex
Pencil (lead-graphite, coloring)
Petroleum jelly (Vaseline)
Phenolphthalein laxatives
   (Ex-Lax)

Play-Doh
Polaroid picture-coating
   fluid
Porous-tip ink marking pens
Prussian blue (ferricyanide)
Putty (less than 2 oz)
Rouge
Rubber cement
Sachets (essential oils, pow-
   der, talc aspiration)
Shampoos (liquid)
Shaving creams and lotions
Soap and soap products
Spackles
Suntan preparation
Sweetening agents (saccha-
   rin, cyclamates)
Teething rings (water sterility)
Thermometers (mercury)
Thyroid tablets (dessicated)
   small amount
Toilet water (alcohol)
Toothpaste (with and without
   fluoride)
Vitamins (without fluoride or
   iron)
Wafarin (under 0.5%)
Water colors
Zinc oxide
Zirconium oxide

Adapted from: *Handbook of Common Poisonings in Children,* 2nd ed., American Academy of Pediatrics, 1983, p. 18.

sent to your local health department. When possible, also check on the paints used for children's toys and dishes.

Plants seem to lure children to explore and taste their lovely leaves, flowers, and fruits. Become familiar with the toxicity of various plants, and select only nontoxic plants for your home. Try to identify the plants already in your yard and your neighborhood and fence off any toxic plants that cannot be removed. Teach your children not to put plants in their mouths and warn older children against eating mushrooms and making brews from plants and flowers. (See Tables 4 to 6.)

TABLE 4
Common Toxic Plants

Akee
Anemone
Autumn crocus
Azalea
Baneberry
Bittersweet
Boxwood
Buttercup
Castor bean
Cherry
Climbing lily
Colocasia (elephant ears)
Daffodil
Daphone
Delphinium
Dieffenbachia (dumb cane)
Foxglove (digitalis)
Hyacinth
Hydrangea
Iris
Jimson weed
Laurel
Lily-of-the-valley

Mistletoe
Mushrooms (various)
Narcissus
Nightshade
Oak
Oleander
Peach
Philodendron
Poinsettia
Poison hemlock
Pokeweed
Potato plant
Ranunculus
Rhododendron
Rhubarb
Rosary pea
Skunk cabbage
Sweet pea
Tobacco
Tomato
Wisteria
Yellow jessamine
Yew

TABLE 5
Common Nontoxic Plants

African violet	Mother-in-law tongue
Aralia false	Peperomia
Begonia	Piggy-back plant
Boston fern	Pilea
Christmas cactus	Pink polka dot plant
Coleus	Plectranthus
Dandelion	Prayer plant
Donkey tail	Rose
Dracaena	Rubber plant (may cause dermatitis)
Hawaiian ti	Schefflera
Hen and chicks	Sensitive plant
Honeysuckle	Snapdragon
Hoya or wax plant	Spider plant
Jade plant	Swedish ivy
Lipstick plant	Violet
Marigold	Wandering Jew
Monkey plant	Weeping fig

Adapted from: *Handbook of Common Poisonings in Children*, 2nd ed., American Academy of Pediatrics, 1983, p. 19.

No matter how carefully you have childproofed your house and yard, and no matter how responsible you think your toddler is, always assume that accidents can happen and be prepared for the possible ingestion of poison. Have a list of emergency telephone numbers, including your child's doctor and the local poison control center number, posted near the phone. Make sure you have syrup of ipecac on hand (to induce vomiting when appropriate). Syrup of ipecac can be purchased without a prescription at most drugstores. Be familiar with the potential poisons in your home so you will know what to do if a poisoning should occur; different poisons require different responses. Learn CPR (cardiopulmonary

TABLE 6
Nontoxic Berries*

Common Name	Color of Berry (Season)
Pyracantha†	Red (autumn and winter)
Dogwood	Red (August to November)
Nandina	Red (summer and autumn)
Barberry	Orange-red (autumn)
	Tan-spotted (winter)
Acouba	Red (autumn)
Mountain ash	Orange (late summer and autumn)
High cranberry	Red (late summer and autumn)

* All other berries should be assumed to be toxic unless identified as being harmless by poison-control personnel.

† May have more poisonous varieties.

Adapted from: *Handbook of Common Poisonings in Children,* 2nd ed., American Academy of Pediatrics, 1983, p. 20.

resuscitation) so you can respond to true emergencies. (See chapter on emergency procedures.)

What should you do if you think that your child has ingested a potential poison?

First: Check for toxic substances and take any pills, plants, or toxic materials out of your child's mouth. Remove anything he might still be holding in his hands.

Second: Carefully look at your child so that when you call your doctor you can report accurately how he seems. Take a minute to evaluate your child's state of alertness and activity. Is he drowsy or unresponsive? Is he overactive? Is he shaking, moving in an unusual way, or convulsing? Check his hands and mouth for chemical burns or stains. Check for drooling and blisters in the mouth, indications of burns of the mouth or throat. Check his breathing. Is he breathing fast or with difficulty? See if his skin feels hot, cold, or sweaty. Look at your child's pupils. Are they unusually small or unusually large? Smell his breath for clues to what he might have ingested.

Third: Try to identify the ingested substance and estimate how much was actually taken. Quickly search the area where your child has been playing. Look for spilled material, extra pills, open containers, or pill bottles.

Finally: If there is any possibility of an ingestion, even if your child looks and acts just fine, *call your child's doctor or your local poison control center.* Often the effects of drugs and other toxins may not show up for several hours. Also, caustic substances may cause burns in the throat that will not be visible on casual inspection.

When you make that call, try to stay calm, but do tell the receptionist that it is an emergency and that you must speak to someone at once. Have the medicine bottle or product container with you at the phone so that you can correctly report the name of the substance that has been swallowed and any other helpful information such as any warnings on the label, the ingredients, the size of the container, and the amount of material remaining in the container. State your child's approximate weight. Remember to tell the person you speak with if your child is taking any medications or suffers from any chronic conditions such as diabetes or epilepsy.

Your doctor or the poison control center will tell you whether or not you should induce vomiting. *Do not induce vomiting if your child is unconscious or having a convulsion, or if the substance ingested is corrosive—such as ammonia, bleach, lye, or sulfuric, nitric, or hydrochloric acid (substances commonly found in drain, oven, and bathroom cleaners). If the substance is a petroleum product, such as gasoline or kerosene or a furniture polish, do not induce vomiting unless specifically directed to, since the substance vomited could get into the lungs and cause an irritation or pneumonia.*

If your child has ingested a corrosive substance or a petroleum product, be prepared to neutralize and dilute the poison with one or two glasses of milk. If you do not have milk, give water or milk of magnesia. The child should be examined by a doctor as soon as possible.

If the identified poison is not corrosive and if you are instructed to induce vomiting, be prepared to give your child the appropriate dose of syrup of ipecac. Ipecac doses are:

- ½ tablespoon up to age 1 year

- 1 tablespoon age 1 to 10 years

- 2 tablespoons greater than 10 years

Always give four to eight ounces of water or juice when giving syrup of ipecac. Do not give milk as it will delay vomiting. A child will usually vomit within twenty minutes. If he doesn't, you may repeat the dose once.

If you do not have syrup of ipecac, you can give your child four to eight ounces of warm water mixed with 2 to 3 teaspoons dishwashing detergent. You can also give clear liquids and subsequently cause vomiting by tickling the back of your child's throat with a blunt object such as a cotton swab or your fingertip.

If you are in a remote area and are unable to contact your doctor or a poison control center, refer to Table 2 to help you determine which commonly ingested poisons are petroleum or corrosive products and should not be vomited. Many home emergency kits contain activated charcoal, which is sometimes used to absorb poison that has been ingested. Never give charcoal to your child without a doctor's advice, since it can be harmful. Also charcoal should not be used at the same time as syrup of ipecac, as it might inhibit the action and the effectiveness of the ipecac and delay vomiting.

If you are instructed to go to the emergency room or to your doctor's office, take along the suspect container, any material the child has already vomited, a vomit bag, and a change of clothes for everyone. When you arrive at the office or the emergency room, you should be received immediately. Give any vomited material you have brought to the nurse or the doctor at once. Depending on what was ingested, the doctor may have the child admitted to the hospital for observation, or treatment may be completed in the emergency room.

Not all poisons are swallowed. Some are splashed on the skin or in the eyes; others are inhaled. If acids, lye, pesticides, or other corrosive or poisonous substances are splashed on the skin, wash the area immediately with lots of soap and water. Remove all contaminated clothing and call your child's doctor or your local poison control center. If the eyes have been splashed, immediately wash them with copious amounts of cool water. Do not use boric acid or eye drops. Wash for ten to fifteen minutes, admittedly not easy to do with a wiggly toddler. If the substance is corrosive, wash for thirty minutes. If you find this difficult, have your child play in the bathtub and repeatedly submerge his head with his eyes open. Call your child's doctor or your local poison control center for further advice. If the material is corrosive, the child should be examined by the doctor even if there is no pain.

When a child is overcome by noxious fumes or gases, such as fuel gases, auto exhaust, leaking household gas, fumes from poisonous chemicals, or the smoke from fires, immediately take him into the fresh air. Loosen any tight clothing and begin artificial respiration. While you are getting air into his lungs, have someone call the doctor or your local poison control center. If the child is comatose or not breathing properly on his own, call your local rescue unit.

Poisoning is one of the leading causes of death and disability in young children. Parents can reduce the chances of poisoning by taking the safety measures we have outlined in this chapter. If a poisoning does occur, parents can increase the chances of their child recovering completely by knowing how to respond calmly, quickly, and appropriately.

Prevention

*T*ry as you may, you can't prevent all the illnesses and mishaps that your child will come across while growing up, but there are some things you can do that will help. Careful attention to immunization, home safety and good health habits will give your family a running start on a safer, healthier life. Here are our suggestions.

Immunizations and Preventive Testing

Immunization is the process by which the body is stimulated to produce antibodies against particular diseases. Vaccines are manufactured from dead or weakened strains of the bacteria or viruses responsible for the illness they seek to prevent and then given by injection or by mouth.

Most pediatricians strongly recommend immunization to protect both individual children and the community at large. As you read about the illnesses these vaccines prevent— illnesses that are now relatively rare but were once quite common—you will understand the importance of mass immunization.

The vaccines routinely given to children in the United States are DPT (for diphtheria, pertussis, and tetanus), OPV (oral polio virus), and MMR (for measles, mumps, and rubella). Recently, vaccines for *Hemophilus influenzae* B have been developed and are being administered by many pediatricians.

Diphtheria, Pertussis, and Tetanus

Diphtheria, a life-threatening illness, was relatively common before the DPT vaccine was introduced in the 1940's. It is still prevalent in countries without strong immunization pro-

TABLE 7
Recommended Routine Childhood Immunizations

Age	Immunization	
2 months	DPT (diphtheria, pertussis, tetanus)	and oral polio
4 months	DPT	and oral polio
6 months	DPT	(and oral polio)
15 months	MMR (measles, mumps, rubella)	
18 months	DPT*	and oral polio
18–60 months	*Hemophilus influenzae* B†	
4 to 6 years	DPT or DT	and oral polio
15 years‡	TD adult tetanus, diphtheria	

* DPT may be given with MMR at 15 months.
† Changes in the composition and schedule of this vaccine are anticipated.
‡ Tetanus immunization should be renewed every ten years.

grams. Both unimmunized and partially immunized individuals can catch diphtheria.

A child infected with diphtheria usually becomes quite ill. A characteristic thick membrane covers the throat and tonsils. Children may die as a result of obstructed breathing, paralyzed muscles, or heart irregularities. Since the illness first affects the nose, throat, and windpipe, it can be transmitted by coughing and sneezing. The incubation period is two to five days, and the illness and its complications may last six weeks or longer. Treatment with antibiotics and antitoxin can kill the bacteria but may not prevent serious complications. If treated, diphtheria is no longer contagious after four days. However, if left untreated, the disease can be contagious for several months.

Pertussis or whooping cough is primarily a respiratory disease. It begins with cold symptoms or a mild cough but becomes more severe over the next two or three weeks. Paroxysms of coughing can be so bad that a child turns red or blue in the face. Eventually, as the coughing fits become more frequent and intense, the characteristic whooping sound is heard as the child gasps for air. Fever, pneumonia, brain inflammation, convulsions, and death may occur, especially in infants less than a year old.

Because of the DPT vaccine, whooping cough has also become relatively rare. However, recent controversy surrounding the side effects of the vaccine has led to a reduction in the number of people immunized. (See below.) A resurgence of the disease has followed: about 1,700 cases of whooping cough are reported each year in the United States. Antibiotics are only moderately successful in eradicating the bacteria, and a lot of careful nursing is needed to pull infants through the illness. Severely affected children typically spend three to four weeks in the hospital being treated to try to prevent brain injury due to lack of oxygen.

Tetanus, also known as lockjaw, comes from a wound. The bacteria that cause the illness live in dirt and enter the body through puncture wounds and cuts. Infected individuals develop severe muscle spasms, which involve the jaw, neck, and vocal cords, and which often lead to death from respiratory failure. Antitoxins and antibiotics are used for treatment.

DPT vaccine immunizes against all three of these devastating illnesses. The immunization schedule varies somewhat from one country to another. In the United States, shots are usually given at two, four, six, and eighteen months and again at five years; in most cases, this schedule is followed even if an infant is underweight or premature. To maintain immunity against tetanus and diphtheria after the initial five DPT inoculations, children and adults need to receive booster shots at least every ten years. The pertussis vaccine, however, is usually not given after age six.

A child may have a severe reaction to any part of the vaccine, but reactions to the pertussis component have raised serious questions. Because the pertussis vaccine is an irritant to nerve tissue, it is most often responsible for the side effects that commonly occur following immunization. Most reactions are mild, typically a slight fever and irritability, usually beginning several hours after the injection and lasting from a few hours to two days. Swelling and redness at the injection site are also common. Giving acetaminophen before the immunization appears to reduce the likelihood of reactions. More severe reactions, such as a temperature over 103 degrees, three hours of high-sustained crying, or convulsions, should be reported to your child's doctor, who may choose to eliminate the pertussis vaccine in future immunizations.

Some reactions appear more often than others, as shown in Table 8. Efforts are being made to produce a vac-

TABLE 8
Frequency of Reactions to DPT Immunization

Reaction	Frequency
Continuously crying, 3 hours or more	1 in 100 immunizations
Temperature of 105 degrees	1 in 500 immunizations
High-pitched, unresponsive cry	1 in 900 immunizations
Convulsions	1 in 2000 immunizations
Reversible neurological problems	1 in 100,000 immunizations
Irreversible neurological problems	1 in 350,000 immunizations

cine with a lower risk of severe side effects; apparently changes in the dosage or the immunizing schedule do not change the probability of a severe reaction. But even though there is some danger from the vaccine, we should not forget that severe consequences from diphtheria, pertussis, and tetanus are far more likely than from the vaccine, and that the likelihood of acquiring the disease increases with each child who goes unimmunized.

Polio

Many of us hardly remember polio or are too young to know that 79,112 cases of paralytic polio were reported in the United States from 1951 through 1955. Polio can be a mild disease with few symptoms or can attack nerve tissue and cause extensive paralysis and permanent damage. Mild cases left victims with nothing worse than a slight limp, but some patients whose chest muscles were paralyzed spent the rest of their lives in an iron lung. Others were unable to speak or swallow. A few people who survived polio seemingly unscathed developed complications years afterward.

The incubation period for polio is three to six days. The paralysis, if it occurs at all, will show up within seven to ten days after exposure to the virus. A child with polio is most contagious shortly before and shortly after the onset of the illness. The virus persists in the throat for about a week, but it can remain in the feces for up to two months. The illness, therefore, can be contagious for quite some time.

Since the development of polio vaccines, this devastating paralytic illness has been virtually eliminated in developed countries. Two vaccines are in use, a "killed" vaccine developed by Dr. Jonas Salk and a "live" vaccine developed by Dr. Albert Sabin.

The Salk vaccine (also termed IPV, inactivated polio vaccine), is used extensively in Europe and offers protection through a series of three primary injections and two boosters. Side effects are rare, usually only a local inflammation at the injection site.

The oral Sabin vaccine is currently preferred in the United States because it is easy to give and very effective in producing high levels of immunity in large communities. This preparation is a live vaccine in which the virus has been weakened enough to produce immunity without inflicting illness. Because it is given orally, it is painless and it has the added advantage that it mimics the route of actual infection. Since the weakened virus is shed through the intestine, it can be spread to others, in a process that has been termed "herd immunity." This is an advantage in places where it is not possible to vaccinate everyone directly. Oral polio vaccine carries a very small risk for others who have no immunity themselves; paralytic polio may develop in unimmunized children exposed to a newly vaccinated child at a rate of 1 in 5 million and in unimmunized adults similarly exposed at a rate of 1 in 1 million. The risk of acquiring paralytic polio from the oral vaccine directly is about 1 in 9 million children. The risk is highest for those with weakened immune systems, but anyone not vaccinated suffers some risk. Therefore children of families immigrating or visiting from less developed lands, where others in the family have not been vaccinated, should not be given the oral vaccine; in such situations, the Salk vaccine is preferable. It should also be given to children with immune deficiency, and to those whose family members are receiving chemotherapy or have immune deficiency.

Measles, Mumps, and Rubella

The combined single immunization known as MMR, for measles, mumps, and rubella, is given at fifteen months of age. (For a discussion of these illnesses see the chapter on common infections. Of course, with the introduction of the vaccine, the illnesses themselves have become much less common.) Like the Sabin polio vaccine, the MMR consists of attenuated (weakened) live virus. Side effects occur in about twenty percent of all children immunized and have the peculiar characteristic of appearing seven to ten days after immunization. Many people thus confuse the fever, irritability, and rash that may result with the actual disease, whereas they are really only symptoms of the body's reaction to the vaccine. More severe reactions, such as arthritis or neck swelling, are quite rare in children. Anyone who has a life-threatening reaction to eggs, however, should not receive this vaccine. In this case, some of its components can be given separately.

Hemophilus influenzae, Type B

This is not "The Flu," which is a viral infection, but a bacterial infection that occasionally causes severe disease such as meningitis, sepsis, and epiglottitis. *Hemophilus influenzae* (sometimes called *H. flu* in medical slang) infections are reviewed in the chapter on infectious diseases.

Recently, a vaccine developed against *Hemophilus influenzae* has been released for general use and recommended by the Academy of Pediatrics for children between the ages of eighteen months to five years. The vaccine currently available is not effective in younger children, and therefore not useful for those at highest risk. It is also not a hundred percent successful in blocking the disease. Side effects are very rare, however, so most doctors recommend the vaccine, especially for children in day care. Vaccines for younger children are now being tested.

Tuberculosis

People are often surprised to learn that we still have tuberculosis in the United States. More than 22,000 cases were reported in 1984, 760 of which involved children less than five years old. The illness is tricky—it can be dormant for many, many years and become active in later life or when a person's immune system is weak. An infected person can then unwittingly spread the bacteria to anyone he comes into close contact with. Crowding, poverty, and malnutrition increase the likelihood of spread in a community, but they are not the only factors, and tuberculosis can rear its head just about anywhere.

The initial infection may go completely unnoticed because the bacterium, which usually settles in the lungs, is isolated by the body's defense mechanisms. It is often picked up as a shadow on a routine x-ray. A secondary spread may occur months later by way of the bloodstream, and can result in infection in other parts of the body causing massively enlarged lymph nodes, meningitis, bone disease, or other problems. A persistent cough may be the first sign of an active infection, especially if accompanied by weakness, weight loss, and night sweating. If you or your children experience any of these symptoms, it is worth checking with your doctor, particularly if you have traveled abroad within the past year or have had close contact with people who are likely to have the disease.

In the United States, a skin test for tuberculosis is performed at regular intervals. Early detection provides the best protection for a child and for his community. A positive skin test means only that a child has come into contact with the bacterium and has reacted to it; it does not mean the child has TB. However, to prevent the spread or late activation of the disease, all children and most adults below age thirty-five who have a positive skin test are treated for the infection. The treatment usually lasts nine to twelve months. A person who is being treated, or who has been treated, for inactive tuberculosis, is not considered contagious. A person who is being treated for active tuberculosis is contagious for some time and should not be in contact with anyone who may be susceptible until his doctor says it is safe.

In some countries where tuberculosis is prevalent, a special vaccine called BCG is given shortly after birth. It is not given in the United States.

Hepatitis

Many viruses can cause liver inflammation which is also called hepatitis. The most common types are hepatitis A and hepatitis B.

Hepatitis A, also termed "infectious hepatitis," is generally transmitted in food and by infected food handlers. It is prevalent in less developed nations, and travelers are therefore at increased risk of infection. Very young children in particular may acquire mild forms of the disease that mimic intestinal flu and therefore go undetected. Older children and adults, however, may develop a more severe illness with nausea, vomiting, malaise, and jaundice (yellow skin).

The incubation period for hepatitis A is two to six weeks. An immune globulin injection given before travel to a high-risk area, or early after exposure, may prevent or modify the illness. Although there was fear at one time that immune globulin might transmit the AIDS virus, we now know that it does not. The period of contagion of hepatitis A is not known, and there is no specific treatment for it.

Hepatitis B, also termed "serum hepatitis," is most often transmitted by blood or bodily fluids. In children transfusions are the most common mode of spread. The incubation period is six weeks to six months. The contagion situation is complicated, however, by the fact that a small percentage of infected individuals, and up to twenty percent of people of Asian ancestry, may be silent carriers of hepatitis B. These people can transmit the illness, and a carrier mother may infect her offspring at birth or afterward during nursing. The child may also become a silent carrier. Hepatitis B carriers have a higher-than-usual risk of subsequent liver problems. For this reason, those at high occupational or other risk for hepatitis B, and newborn infants of carrier mothers, are immunized with a new vaccine (HB). In the immediate newborn period the babies also receive a specific form of immune globulin (HBIG).

Home Safety

It is a sad fact that every year in the United States about 4,800 children under the age of four die because of accidents. Most of these accidents could have been prevented. Two of the most effective ways to promote safety are to anticipate hazards and to teach safety by parental example and consistent limit-setting.

It is important to understand your child's abilities and developmental phases in order to know how best to protect him. For example, injuries to a newborn baby often happen in automobile accidents if the infant is not properly secured in a car seat. A baby can also be hurt by falling from the arms of someone—often a young sibling—carrying him.

No sooner are these dangers past than the next set of problems must be anticipated. Babies may start to scoot at two months of age and roll over by four to five months. It is best to leave infant seats on the floor and not in the middle of the table or on countertops. When reaching to get diapers, keep a hand—and an eye—on the baby lying on the changing table.

At four to five months of age, babies explore their environment by putting objects in their mouths. Parents must then keep anything that might cause an infant to choke or suffocate out of his reach.

From six to fourteen months of age, the big changes are in babies' ability to move about. They begin to sit, crawl, pull up, cruise, and walk. This alters both the range of what they can grasp and the speed and accuracy with which they can reach tempting objects. New hazards arise such as drowning in water accidently left in the tub, getting a burn from heater grills or hot tap water, and swallowing or choking on a variety of treasures swept into forgotten corners or buried in carpets. Children often swallow things like coins, pins, and small beads, which can be dangerous though rarely poisonous. Most of these objects cause little harm unless they get stuck in a child's trachea and hamper breathing. If your child has swallowed such an object and has trouble breathing, starts to wheeze, or passes blood in his stool, call your doctor. Parents should in any case familiarize themselves with CPR procedures for choking.

Because they dislike being restrained, children at this age may balk at being placed in their car seats or play pens. Parents must now be firm and absolutely consistent in enforcing the rules that affect their child's safety.

Little adventurers between one and three years of age are fascinated by door knobs, lids, bottles, tools, and the like. Children in this age group often feel that anything in a jar, bottle, or can is fair game for eating and drinking. For this reason, it's a good idea always to have on hand syrup of ipecac (see chapter on poisoning).

Four- and five-year-olds are often fearless and frequently oblivious to danger. An interest in water play may lead to exploration of a swimming pool, or a passion for trucks may result in an impulsive dash for the street, so you should begin now to teach your child about safety, particularly traffic safety. When crossing the street, carry your small child, or hold his hand or have him hold on to your clothes or to the stroller, and don't permit your child to cross the street unaccompanied before age seven.

Toys may pose dangers for children of all ages. Recently toy manufacturers have made an effort to indicate the age-appropriateness of their products and have issued warnings when a particular toy has proved unsafe. However, there are still some hazardous goodies out there. Some toys have sharp edges or points, while others may have easily detachable small parts or dangerous mechanisms. And remember that a toddler can do some awful things with his older sibling's toys! For older children tricycles or bicycles, skateboards, and rickety play structures can be safety hazards.

Children who see their parents always using seat belts and helmets are more likely to do the same. If parents are relaxed about taking medicines, their children may be more inclined to try to swallow pills. Remind your child that pills are not candy every time you administer them. Smoking poses several hazards: the smoke is passively inhaled, matches are a fire hazard, and cigarette butts are toxic if ingested. And, of course, a child, learning by example, may eventually want to try smoking, too.

General Precautions in the Home

❑ Keep smoke detectors in working condition and fire extinguishers charged.

❑ Cover all electrical outlets, either with commercial plastic plugs or with tape. Secure all extension and other electrical cords by tacking or taping them to the wall or floor. Secure all lamps and unplug hair dryers, irons, and other appliances when not in use. Never overload circuits or fuses.

❑ Protect against burns by lowering the hot water heater thermostat to 120 degrees or low. Cover heat registers or grills with shields made of narrowly spaced dowels.

❑ Use (but don't totally rely on) safety locks and latches. Some toddlers are very skilled at breaking and entering! Be sure that you can close and lock doors, but that your child cannot lock himself inside a room or a closet.

❑ Secure all medicines (including aspirin, vitamins, and iron pills) in a locked box or cabinet. Do the same with furniture polish, household cleansers and the like. Never leave these cabinets unlocked to run into another room for "just a minute." Discard all medications not in current use by flushing them down the toilet.

☐ Have frequent clean-up patrols to put away toys and retrieve objects that could be dangerous.

☐ Cover coffee table corners and all sharp edges with foam rubber or cloth. Walk around your house and see which objects are at your child's eye level and could be dangerous.

☐ Conduct regular fire and/or earthquake drills with older children.

☐ Remove poisonous plants from the house. (See the list of common toxic plants in the chapter on poisoning.)

☐ Check your house, especially if it is an older one, for peeling, exposed old paint on walls and furniture. It may be lead-based and very dangerous. To locate an appropriate testing facility, consult the environmental protection agency in your area. Asbestos insulations or acoustic tiles, if present, should be removed only by professionals expert in handling hazardous wastes.

Additional precautions to take in each room:

Child's Bedroom

☐ Place tot-finder decals on windows to alert firefighters to the presence of a child.

☐ Make sure that crib slats are no more than 2½ inches apart and that bumper pads are in place. Toys that stretch across the crib should be removed at night. When a child can climb out of his crib, he should begin to sleep in a bed with safety rails.

❑ Put a side rail on a child's first bed or pad the floor around the bed.

❑ Secure the top and bottom of bunk beds and make sure safety rails are always in place. The area around the beds should always be clear of toys and debris. A ladder should be attached to the side or end of the bed.

❑ Keep all plastic bags, such as dry cleaners' bags, and all small objects that could be swallowed out of the room.

❑ Be sure your child cannot get trapped inside toy chests. Also, modify toy chests so that the lid cannot fall on your child's head.

Bathroom

❑ Lock up all medicines and cleansers and keep them out of reach of children at all times.

❑ Use a rubber bathtub mat in the tub to help you and your children avoid slipping when climbing into the tub.

❑ Never leave your child in a bath alone until he can swim.

❑ Keep all electrical appliances unplugged and out of reach.

Kitchen

❑ Begin to teach your child the meaning of "hot" at age nine months.

❑ Do not work at the stove holding an infant in your arms. Do not position an infant seat near the stove.

❑ Keep furniture, including stools, away from the stove.

❑ Place a smoke detector in the kitchen and have a charged fire extinguisher on hand. If a grease fire occurs, put it out by smothering it with a pot lid or a towel, *not with water.*

❑ Unplug and store all small electrical appliances when they are not in use.

❑ Use splatter covers when frying food and turn all pot handles toward the back of the stove when cooking.

❑ Consider removing knobs from burners when not in use.

❑ Always return knives or other sharp and dangerous objects to drawers and cabinets that are out of your child's sight and reach.

❑ Store all household chemicals, cleansers, and insect repellants in locked cupboards. Avoid putting these items under the sink, even if the cabinet handles are secured with a "child-proof" lock.

❑ Make the trash inaccessible.

Living Room

❑ Secure mirrors and bookcases by bolting them to the wall or floor.

❑ Avoid glass or stone coffee tables and cover any sharp edges with foam rubber or cloth.

❑ Place a screen that only you can remove in front of the fireplace; never leave a fire unattended.

❑ Block off all floor and wall heaters or construct protective grills to keep children away from them.

❑ Tack down electrical cords and unplug them when not in use.

❑ When guests leave, remove nuts, vegetable dips, and any small objects on which a baby might choke.

❑ Put decals at your child's eye level on all large glass doors and windows so that he will not run into the glass.

❑ Screen off balconies and be certain your child cannot climb onto railings and banisters using nearby furniture!

❑ Secure any windows accessible to your child by latching or screening them, but make sure they can be opened from the outside in case of fire. Make it a rule to open double-hung windows *only from the top*.

Stairs

❑ Install safety gates that meet current standards at both the top and bottom of every stairwell. Older models may have slats (to climb on) or open crisscrossed surfaces (to trap a child's neck) and are not safe!

❑ Keep the stairs well lit. Do not use them as a play area. Teach your child to negotiate the stairs first by crawling down backward and later by walking down holding the handrail.

❑ Remove hazardous objects from the stairs. Make it a habit to keep stairs *clear*.

❑ Block openings between the balusters of your stairs with plastic mesh or chicken wire until your child uses the handrail with confidence.

You may begin to feel that your house has a rather grim, stripped-for-battle look. Keep in mind that most of the recommended measures are temporary—your children won't be toddlers very long.

Garage and Workroom

❑ Keep your garage or workroom locked and close the door behind you when working there. Do not let your child play in these areas alone.

❑ Put all chemicals, paints, and insecticides in labeled, tightly closed containers and lock them away where your child cannot reach them.

❑ Put all tools, nuts, bolts, and nails out of reach.

❑ Cover electrical outlets and unplug all power tools when not in use.

❑ Remove or lock the doors of any unused refrigerators or cabinets that could be tempting hiding places.

Garden and Indoor Plants

❑ Be aware of any toxic plants inside your house that cannot be removed and teach your child about them. (See chapter on poisoning.)

❑ Identify all plants in your garden and remove or isolate those that are toxic before an accidental ingestion occurs. Refrain from planting toxic plants such as azaleas, rhododendrons, and daffodils until your child is old enough to understand that they are dangerous to eat— about six years old. (See chapter on poisoning for a list of common plants that are toxic.)

❑ Teach your child not to eat plants and discourage making wildflower teas and sucking nectar even from familiar, nontoxic plants.

❑ Teach your child to avoid picking and eating mushrooms. (It takes considerable expertise to identify the safe kind correctly.)

❑ Teach your child not to chew on necklaces and other jewelry made from seeds, beans, or grasses. Consider getting rid of these attractive nuisances.

❑ Do not use insecticides that leave residues harmful to human beings or pets.

Yard Safety

❑ Enclose your yard so that your child cannot wander off and strangers cannot wander in.

☐ Get rid of anything your child might get trapped in such as unused cabinets, refrigerators, drain pipes, or sheds.

☐ Make sure all play equipment—swings, slides, seesaws —meets current safety standards and is appropriate for your child's age. The Consumer Product Safety Commission constantly updates the safety of such equipment. The current telephone number is (800) 638-2772. Reevaluate your equipment periodically as your child grows.

☐ Enclose and seal off a swimming pool or pond. No child should play near water without constant parental supervision.

☐ Keep yard tools and insecticides out of reach. Do not use toxic compounds such as snail bait.

Automobile Safety

☐ Use your seat belt and insist that all passengers, large or small, buckle up, too. Children under age four should be in a car seat. Children learn by example!

☐ Never allow a baby to travel in a car bed or on someone's lap.

☐ Allow extra time for your trip so you can pull over and wait if there is too much distraction or disruption in the car.

☐ Use door safety locks.

☐   Do not permit children to hold their hands or toys out of the window.

☐   No matter how rushed you are, always be sure that the car keys and the baby are out before you lock car doors!

Some effort is needed to create a safe environment for infants, toddlers, and young children, but it's worth it. Preventing an accident is a lot easier than dealing with an emergency.

Habits for Good Health

Many parents want to know what they can do to keep their child healthy. They often ask "Does my child need vitamins?" and "How much sleep does he need to keep from being run down?" Their concerns usually involve clothing, sleep, diet, hygiene, and exercise—and rightfully so. Good health depends on the proper care of the body and children should be taught good health habits as soon as they are old enough to care for themselves. The patterns established during childhood are often habits for life!

It is not always easy to teach children good health habits. Everyone must realize that good health habits may be hard to attain in the hectic twentieth century. In fact, it may be particularly hard for today's parents, whose own needs and schedules understandably provide little time for observing their children's natural patterns. When both parents work away from the home, their routines may actually come into conflict with those of their children. Bedtime may be delayed if Dad gets home late and wants some family time. Breakfast may be rushed if Mom has to catch a commuter bus. A quick canned or frozen dinner looks good to harried working parents.

Parents are exposed to a lot of advice, some good and some bad. Suggestions may come from relatives, total strangers, or the news media, and they are often eagerly accepted by parents who are anxious to "do the right thing." "Tammy hasn't had a single cold since I've made sure she has a little garlic at least once a week," says one parent. Another adds, "I don't understand why Peter keeps getting colds. I give him vitamins every day, even extra vitamin C." How can we determine which health practices really do make a difference, which are really worth the effort?

We hope to help sort out fact from fiction, good hygiene from nitpicking. Above all, we wish to stress that good health habits ought not to become battle zones between parents and their children.

Let's begin with clothing and body temperature. The human body responds automatically to maintain its correct temperature. When we are cold, we shiver to retain heat. When we are hot, we sweat, which lowers our temperature by evaporation. Clothes should assist the body in this process, not impede it. Here are some rough guidelines. Layered clothing allows adjustments to be made during the day as temperatures rise and fall. Wool and polypropelene provide warmth while still allowing moisture to escape. Cotton is an ideal fabric for hot climates because it acts like a wick to draw off moisture.

Hats or hoods are useful in winter because a lot of the body's heat can be lost from the head. They also protect people from sun exposure. The trick is to get kids to wear them! Gloves or mittens are really necessary when it is wet and cold, because fingers are particularly sensitive. To best accomplish their function, gloves and mittens should contain wool or polypropelene.

You might also pay some attention to your choice of colors in clothing, not only for aesthetic value, but for practical purposes. For example, bright colors such as yellow and red make your child more visible in crowds. On the other hand, these same colors may attract wasps and bees on a hike. Black tends to absorb heat while white tends to reflect it.

How do you dress children when they are ill? It is very tempting to bundle them up and pile on the covers when they are having chills. But while it may make them feel better, it can also raise their temperature, which in turn can make them feel worse. We therefore recommend that a child with a fever be lightly dressed. Having said all this, please remember that these principles are only meant as guidelines and should not be applied rigidly!

Shoes are another topic of concern for parents. "When do you need to buy the first pair?" "What kind of shoes provide the best support?" Well, here is what is known about children's shoes. The primary purpose of shoes is protection. Babies, therefore, do not need shoes at all until they walk. In fact, the little sleepers with foot coverings sometimes cause rashes and inflammation of the toes. Once toddlers are walking, the best shoe is a light one with a flexible sole. High tops are recommended only if children habitually kick off their shoes. The need for "support" is a fallacy—children need to *use* their foot muscles to strengthen them. Shoes should be adequately wide. As it is, toes and toenails need a lot of attention to avoid troublesome infections, peeling skin, blisters, cracks, and athlete's foot. Tight-fitting, stiff shoes tend to constrict motion and cramp the foot. Since children's shoes can be very expensive, parents may be relieved to know that regular children's sneakers satisfy most of the requirements listed above. For children whose feet sweat a great deal, leather may be a better choice than plastic or rubber. Children who wear sneakers should ideally have several pairs so that they can be left to air and dry out. Sandals are most comfortable for the summer. Rain boots in wet climates are useful to avoid that cold, clammy feeling, but children should be able to remove them once they are indoors.

Sleep is a subject that invariably arouses the passions of parents, grandparents, and children. How much sleep do children need? What if a toddler skips naps and acts cranky in the evening? Is a routine bed time essential?

There are no simple answers to these questions. On the whole, children get as much sleep as they need. The normal range is very wide; some children simply require much less sleep than others. The fact is that children fall asleep when they are tired.

When children first drop their daytime naps, they may go through a period of bizarre sleep patterns. Sometimes they collapse early in the evening and then wake up at an ungodly hour early in the morning, full of beans and ready to play. This is not harmful to the child, even though it may be inconvenient and annoying to their parents.

Most pediatricians do not recommend strict scheduling and forced naps. Nevertheless, after you have observed and assessed your child's physical needs, you can help him to establish regular sleep patterns by putting him to bed every night at the same time with sleep rituals that both you and he can count on. Although you don't want to make going to bed an unpleasant experience, you also don't want to let your child prolong the evening beyond what seems reasonable.

Advice about sleep is outdone only by advice about food! Children do not eat at all like adults. They will often eat the same thing day after day. It is not unusual for parents to tell us their child exists on nothing but peanut butter and jelly sandwiches. Children also have no trouble eating dessert before the main course. Parents want to know to what extent their children's food choices are appropriate and when they should interfere. Is it a good idea to force children to eat their vegetables or finish what is on their plate? What is the social importance of mealtime for toddlers, and might this be destroyed by too much emphasis on being a "good eater?"

It's relatively easy to provide an infant with a nutritious diet. Breast milk is the most appropriate food for infants. The fat, carbohydrate, protein, and mineral composition is particularly well suited to their needs. Vitamins, though not present in high quantities, are fully absorbed by the infant. In fact, the mother has to be seriously ill or malnourished before the breast-fed infant will develop any measurable deficiency. There seems to be little evidence that vitamin supplements are necessary; on the other hand, infant vitamins in proper doses are not harmful. Some physicians also advocate giving extra fluoride to protect the teeth, while others feel that the small amount transmitted in breast milk is sufficient.

Formulas are nutritionally adequate, and many a healthy baby has been bottle-fed in infancy. Allergic reactions to cow's milk or to soy products are always a possibility, however. Since solids are introduced slowly, babies continue to derive a major part of their nutritional needs from breast milk or formula for some time; their acceptance or rejection of certain solids, their likes and dislikes, are therefore not very critical. At this age, learning to enjoy mealtime may well be much more important than eating a balanced diet.

The real challenge comes when children begin to feed themselves. By the time they are toddlers many children have developed strong food preferences and they often eat only one to two meals a day, consuming what seems to us to be very small portions. Fortunately, children don't need three square meals a day to be well-nourished. Parents should feel reassured if looking back over several days or weeks they can see that their child has eaten a variety of foods from the major food groups. Even small quantities of meat, fish, yogurt, cheese, green and yellow vegetables, and fruit should provide all the nourishment that a child needs for growth.

It is important to watch that your child is getting enough iron and calcium and that he is not consuming excessive amounts of milk or juice. Iron stores begin to decline after a baby is six months old. Children who don't get enough iron in their diet may suffer a variety of consequences including listlessness, reduced appetite, irritability, anemia, and possibly diminished mental functioning. The little cherub who always drinks his bottle of milk may be iron-deficient. Milk contains virtually no iron and tends to diminish the appetite when consumed in large quantities. An iron-fortified formula helps, but iron-fortified cereals are a good early source of iron. Once a child is eating a varied diet, good amounts of iron can come from red meat, spinach, broccoli, blackstrap molasses, raisins, and red and navy beans. Vegetarians and those who don't eat red meat need to be especially conscious of the need for adequate iron.

Calcium is of particular interest today, since there is now some evidence that consuming adequate dietary calcium during childhood can influence bone strength in adult women. We are frequently asked how much is enough? If children are consuming at least an average of eight ounces of milk products a day, we do not advise additional calcium. For children who are allergic to milk, a variety of calcium supplements are available, and your child's doctor will advise you about whether and when to use them.

Although fruits contain many healthy nutrients, it is a misconception that fruit juices are particularly healthful. Though many contain vitamins and are delicious on the whole, juices are nutritionally deficient thirst quenchers. The sugar content may damage teeth, especially if a bottle is slowly sucked all day long or during the night. A bottle of water with just a dash of juice for color will accomplish the same end! For the toddler who drinks from a cup, a little juice can be a nice treat, but too much juice may diminish his appetite for more nutritious foods.

Providing a varied diet is relatively easy, but getting a child to consume one may be more difficult. Babies and toddlers have strong textural preferences and teething or the lack of teeth can also limit what they will eat. Older children may have a heightened sensitivity to smells and spices, as well as strong tastes that can lead to many food aversions.

Parents learn early on that there is little you can do to force a child to eat—and there is little you *should* do. Certainly you should try to make the food as wholesome and appealing as possible. Trying different textures and combinations can help. Foods that are rejected in one form may be palatable in another. Peas, for example, bought fresh and cooked to make them soft, may be rejected by a child who finds their taste and texture mealy and unappealing. This same child might like frozen peas that have been slightly thawed, because they are sweeter and have a less starchy taste. Other variations you might try are chicken soup with peas, an egg-yolk omelet with peas, or stir-fried rice and chicken with peas. After all this, your child might still detect and turn down peas in every form, but at least you have tried and can then move on to another vegetable.

There is no point in having a fixed idea about the amount of food a child should eat. Since metabolic requirements vary widely from one child to the next, and from one stage in the child's growth to the next, there is no right amount that is valid for all. From infancy onward, most children who have not been cajoled or coerced into some abnormal feeding pattern will adjust the quantity of their food intake according to what they need. At times they may eat only a few bites, and at others consume more than their parents. Again, as long as their diet is varied, there is no need to worry.

The major eating problem, however, is usually not the amount consumed but the love of unhealthy delectibles. The food industry has chosen to market its products with the same type of seductive advertising used for other consumer goods. The main goal is to appeal to the young, even at the expense of nutritional value. The result is often junk food loaded with sugar, salt, chemical flavors, and artificial coloring. Food manufacturers often try to increase a product's appeal to the young by providing little prizes in the package, making it almost irresistible. Some children want to eat nothing but soda pop, candy, and potato chips. Under these circumstances, providing good nutrition is an even greater challenge and responsibility! One thing parents can do is to teach by example. It's better to fill the refrigerator with delicious fruits than with junk food. It is hard for a child not to crave soda pop if it's always available. Tasty foods that have minimal nutritional value, such as sweet desserts, candy, and undiluted fruit juice, should never be given as a substitute for a meal just so a child "will eat something." Nor do they belong in a lunch box. On the other hand, a cookie, fruit roll, or granola bar will not harm a child—and may also prevent some unfortunate food cravings later on in life. Parents can blend limit-setting with negotiation and accommodation by making a reasonable offer and sticking to it. This way, the child will not feel totally thwarted and will come to appreciate that his nutritional well-being is an appropriate parental concern.

A word about drugs, drinking, and smoking. In these areas, especially, parental example can establish the principles of moderation and self-protection. Children absorb the actions and motivations of their parents and are likely to follow similar patterns. Therefore, smokers often beget smokers; drinkers often beget drinkers. A casual attitude at home about drugs may engender a similar attitude on the part of the child. When parents are nonchalant to the point of indifference, the children may follow suit.

Cleanliness is certainly a health habit worth encouraging but we should be clear on what is required for health as opposed to what is enjoyable or pleasing. For example, some babies love a bath while others despise every aspect of it. In fact, water is not all that good for the skin, because it tends to dry it out. Soaps also remove surface oil, and the result may be a form of eczema or dry itchy skin rash. We often face the unenviable task of trying to convince a parent whose child loves his daily bath that his skin would prefer one every third or fourth day. As children grow older, however, the reverse problem may arise. Taking a bath may not be their favorite thing to do, and children often need to be reminded to wash with water *and* soap.

As soon as children are old enough, they should be taught to clean themselves properly after using the bathroom to keep stool from entering their genital area. Careful toilet habits and daily change of underwear are important to good health. These practices can prevent skin and genital infections and they deserve the earliest and most consistent parental attention. Children should also be taught how to clean and trim their nails, and brush and floss their teeth.

When children are too young to brush their teeth effectively, parents should wipe their teeth daily with a moist, slightly rough washcloth to remove sugars and acids. Most toddlers love to imitate their parents and siblings, and when they are around fifteen months old they can be given a small, soft toothbrush. No toothpaste is needed, though it will not harm the toddler who insists upon it. Brushing at this age is merely to gain experience and start the ritual. Parents should continue to wipe or brush their children's teeth until they are three or four years old, even as children learn to care for their teeth themselves. Some children prefer to hear a story or lie on their parent's lap while their teeth are brushed. Especially cooperative youngsters will allow their teeth to be flossed.

Most city water contains enough fluoride to be effective in the prevention of cavities. If you don't live in the city, check with your dentist to see if fluoride supplements are recommended in your area. Also, if you use bottled water, check the concentration of fluoride. A good time for children to meet the dentist is between the ages of three and four. Most children will allow the dentist to peek into their mouths and count their teeth. If you or your pediatrician are concerned about the condition of your child's teeth, you can certainly take your child earlier.

In addition to cleaning those teeth, try not to give your children an abundance of sweet sticky foods. Honey and raisins are as sticky as candy and cake. Please avoid giving juice in a bed-time bottle as the sugars and the acid can destroy tooth enamel. Many dentists advise that once a child has teeth, prolonged sucking at the breast or from a bottle should be avoided. If a child must take his bottle to bed with him, make sure it is out of his mouth once he is asleep. Most dentists prefer that children be weaned from bottles and pacifiers by age two, but a decision to wean may depend on factors other than your child's dental health.

What about exercise? Parents certainly have a responsibility to guide their children to wholesome play that does not endanger them. On the other hand, children vary in athletic ability and interest. Adults need to take care neither to inhibit their children because of their own fears nor to project their own expectations on their children. It is best to give children plenty of time outdoors and a variety of age-appropriate activities to choose from. The chance to explore, move, and play is a wonderful gift of childhood, and it should be enjoyed fully. Many a parent will also rediscover the child within himself if he joins, but does not intrude upon, the outdoor play of his children. What about playing outdoors in bad weather? It may come as a surprise that there is actually no scientific evidence that inclement weather is a factor in childhood illness. We suggest that, in general, children should be out even if the weather is not very good. Of course, if it's cold or wet, dress them appropriately; they will certainly be more comfortable.

Our best advice is to relax. Children are sturdy and resilient creatures, and they neither require nor benefit from rigid do's and don't's. As long as love, good will, and flexibility are present, the rules parents do set for their children are likely to lead to a lifetime of good health habits.

Appendix: Emergency Procedures

Some emergencies are bound to happen in every household. Children learn by exploring, and it sometimes gets them into trouble. It is important for you and for anyone else taking care of a child to know what to do in an emergency and how to do it.

Be prepared in advance, so that you can react quickly and appropriately in an emergency. Have emergency telephone numbers handy and keep them up to date. The first aid kit and home pharmacy should be stocked at all times, and you, as well as any caretakers, should know where they are and how to use them.

In this section, we review the basic approaches to the most common and urgent problems you are likely to encounter. Refer back to the appropriate chapters for more information. If reading the section straight through makes you feel a little weak, remember that you won't have all of these problems at once, and you may be lucky enough to escape almost all of them. We hope that reading the information will give you confidence to face an emergency, and help you do the right thing if one arises.

This Appendix was adapted from material prepared by the American Academy of Pediatrics and the American Heart Association.

CPR: Cardiopulmonary Resuscitation

When is CPR (cardiopulmonary resuscitation) needed? What are the steps to go through? Remember the ABCs: Airway, Breathing, and Circulation. CPR is called for if the airway is blocked, breathing is halted, or circulation is interrupted. Deal with each of those components in turn. But if the airway is clear, the child is breathing, and pulse is continuing, CPR is not necessary. For example, if a child has fainted or has had a convulsion, but is breathing and has no signs of obstruction of the breathing passages, CPR is not called for. Similarly, there is no need to intervene if a child has some signs of choking but is coughing well and able to speak.

Airway

Signs of an obstructed airway (choking) include increasing difficulty in breathing, with an ineffective cough, an inability to speak or cry, crowing respirations, and bluish skin color. If you suspect true obstruction, follow these steps:

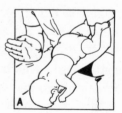

Infant less than one year old

- Place infant face down over your arm with his head lower than his body. Rest your arm on your thigh.
- Give 4 rapid, moderate blows between the shoulder blades, as in picture A.

- If the infant is still not breathing, roll him over and give 4 rapid chest compressions. See CPR picture E.
- If he is still not breathing, alternate between 4 back blows and 4 chest compressions.

Child one to eight

- Place the child on his back and kneel next to him.
- Put the heel of your hand on the middle of his abdomen, between the rib cage and the belly button (see picture B). Give 6 to 10 rapid inward and upward thrusts (Heimlich maneuver).

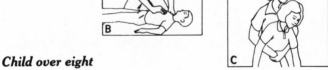

Child over eight

- Use two-handed Heimlich maneuver, with the child standing, sitting, or lying down; see picture C.

If these measures are ineffective, try sweeping the inside of the mouth with your finger while you hold the tongue down with your thumb. Call for help while you continue CPR.

Breathing

If the child is unresponsive and not breathing:

- First, clear the child's throat and wipe out any fluid. Next, place him on his back.

- Straighten his neck (unless you suspect a neck injury) and lift his jaw as shown in picture D.
- With a baby, blow gently into the nose and mouth. Be sure to form a tight seal around both, so that you will inflate the victim's lungs slightly. With a larger child, pinch the nostrils closed and breathe into the mouth.

- Breathe at a rate of 20 breaths a minute (one breath every 3 seconds) for infants, and 15 breaths a minute (one every 4 seconds) for children.
- Use just enough air to move the chest up and down.

Circulation

If there is no pulse or heartbeat, CPR must include cardiac support:

- Shake the child to check responsiveness.
- Look for chest motion.
- Feel for a pulse at the inside of the elbow.

If there is no responsiveness, breath, or pulse, follow these steps:

- Clear the airway and begin mouth-to-mouth breathing.
- Place the child on his back on a firm surface.

- For an infant, using two fingers
  (see picture E), depress the
  breastbone ½ to 1 inch at the
  level of the nipples, 100 times
  a minute. Meanwhile, give
  one breath for every 5 heart
  compressions.

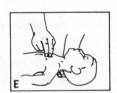

- For a child more than a year old, using the heel of the
  hand, depress the lower third of the breastbone 1 to
  1½ inches, 80 times per minute. Again, give one
  breath for every 5 heart compressions.

First Aid for Other Emergencies

**Never give food or drink to any severely
injured patient!**

Poisoning

First steps:

- Separate the patient and the poison.
- Always call a poison control center, doctor, or hospital
  emergency room promptly.

The following are safe first-aid measures for various
types of poisonings.

Swallowed Poisons

When a child has swallowed a poison, it is an emergency—any nonfood substance is potentially a poison. Call a doctor, poison-control center, or hospital emergency department *promptly* for advice.

Do *not* make the patient vomit if:

- He is unconscious or drowsy.
- He is convulsing or having tremors (or twitching of the arms or legs) or uncontrolled body movements.
- He has swallowed a strong corrosive, such as a drain cleaner, oven cleaner, toilet-bowl cleaner, or strong acid.
- He has swallowed furniture polish, kerosene, gasoline, or other petroleum products.

Otherwise, make the patient vomit, to get the unabsorbed poison out of the system:

- Give syrup of ipecac—not salt water.
- For a child under one year, give 1½ teaspoons of syrup of ipecac.
- For a child from one year to ten years old, give 3 teaspoons (or 1 tablespoon, or ½ oz) syrup of ipecac, followed by 4 to 8 oz of water. If child does not vomit within 20 minutes, you may repeat the dose *once only*.
- For a child over ten, give 2 tablespoons (1 oz) syrup of ipecac, followed by 4 to 8 oz of water.

If so instructed, drive carefully to a medical facility. Take a pan to collect the vomitus. Also bring the container the ingested material came in, with label intact, or whatever left-over material there is. Proper treatment depends on knowing exactly what the toxin is.

Inhaled poisons

Inhaled poisons include fuel gases, auto exhaust, dense smoke from fires, and fumes from poisonous chemicals.

- Get the victim into fresh air.
- Loosen his clothing.
- If victim is not breathing, start artificial respiration promptly. Do not stop until the patient is breathing well or until help arrives.
- Have someone else call a doctor, poison-control center, hospital, or rescue unit.
- Transport victim to a medical facility promptly.

Poison in Eye

- Holding lids open, flush out the eye immediately with water.
- Remove any contact lenses.
- Irrigate eye for 15 minutes, with a continuous, gentle stream of water from a pitcher.
- Never permit eye to be rubbed. Do not use eye drops.
- Call doctor, poison-control center, or emergency department for further advice.

Poison on the Skin

- If the poison is dry, brush it off gently.
- Immediately wash off the skin with a large amount of water and soap.
- Remove contaminated clothing.

- Call doctor, poison-control center, or emergency department for further advice.

Bites and Stings

Snakebite

NONPOISONOUS

- Treat as a puncture wound (see under Skin Wounds below).
- Consult a doctor.

POISONOUS

- Put the patient and the injured part at rest. Keep patient —and yourself—quiet.
- Do not apply ice directly to skin. Use cool compresses for pain.
- Sucking the wound may be beneficial, but do not make any incisions.
- Take victim promptly to a medical facility.
- If you cannot get to medical help within an hour, apply a constricting band (loose enough to allow two fingers under it) above the bite, but not around fingers or toes.

Insect Bites

Dangerous bites can include those of spiders, scorpions, or unusual reactions to other stinging insects such as bees, wasps, hornets, etc.

- For a scorpion sting, get immediate medical advice.
- For spider bites, obtain medical advice. Save a live specimen of spider if possible.
- For other insect bites, remove the stinger by scraping the skin with a plastic card or fingernail. Do not pull it out.

Then, in all cases,

- Use cold compresses on the bite area to relieve pain.
- If the victim stops breathing, use artificial respiration and have someone call a rescue unit or a doctor for further instructions.
- If there are any reactions such as hives, generalized rash, pallor, weakness, collapse, nausea, vomiting, or tightness in the chest, nose, or throat, get the patient to a doctor or emergency department immediately.

Ticks

After any walk in the woods, inspect a child carefully for ticks. They carry dangerous diseases and must be completely removed.

- Use protected fingers or tweezers placed close to the tick's head to pull it away from the victim's skin.
- If the tick's head breaks off, the child should be taken without delay for medical removal.

Animal Bites

- Wash the wound gently but thoroughly with soap and water for 15 minutes.

- Call a doctor or medical facility for advice. Bats, raccoons, skunks, and foxes often carry rabies, and if a cat or dog bites without provocation, the possibility of rabies should be considered. In either case, treatment to prevent rabies may be needed.

Burns and Scalds

Protection against tetanus should be considered in all burns.

Small Heat Burns

- Immerse burns in cool water for 10 to 15 minutes, or apply cool (50 to 60 degrees) compresses to burns for pain relief.
- Do not apply ointments, greases, powder, etc.
- Do not break blisters.
- Nonadhesive material such as household aluminum foil makes an excellent emergency covering for burns.
- Burns of any size on the face, hands, feet, or genitals should be seen immediately by a doctor.

Extensive Burns

- Keep patient lying flat.
- Try to remove clothing from burn area—but if not easily removed, leave it alone.
- Apply cool wet compresses to injured area (not to more than 25% of the body at one time).
- Keep patient warm.
- Get patient to hospital or doctor at once.

Electrical Burns

- Disconnect power source or pull the victim away from source using wood or cloth. Do *not* touch the victim with bare hands while he is in contact with power source.
- Electric shock may require CPR.
- All electrical burns must be evaluated by a physician.

Skin Wounds

Protection against tetanus should be considered whenever the skin is broken.

Bruises

Apply cold compress for half hour (no ice next to skin). If skin is broken, treat as a cut. For injuries caused by catching a hand or foot in bicycle spokes, always consult physician without delay.

Scrapes

Use wet gauze or cotton to sponge off gently with clean water and soap. Apply sterile dressing, preferably nonadhesive or "film" type (Telfapad).

Cuts

SMALL: Wash with clean water and soap. Hold under running water. Apply sterile gauze dressing.

LARGE: Apply dressing. Press firmly and elevate to stop bleeding—use tourniquet only if necessary to control bleeding. Bandage. Secure medical care. Do not use iodine or other antiseptics without medical advice.

Puncture Wounds

Consult physician.

Splinters

Wash with water and soap. Remove with tweezers or forceps. Wash again. If a splinter is not easily removed, consult physician.

Fractures

If a child's injured limb is deformed, it is probably broken; splint the limb before moving the child. If you suspect a neck or back injury, don't move the child without medical assistance.

Sprains

Elevate injured part and apply only *cold* compresses. If marked pain or swelling present, seek medical advice.

Teeth

Knocked-Out Tooth

- If the tooth is dirty, rinse it gently in running water. Do not scrub it.
- Gently insert the tooth in gum and hold it in its socket. If this is not possible, place it in a container of milk or cool water.
- Go immediately to your dentist (within thirty minutes, if possible). Don't forget to bring the tooth.

Broken tooth

- Gently clean dirt or debris from the injured area with warm water.
- Place cold compresses on the face near the injured tooth to minimize swelling.
- Go to the dentist immediately.

Eyes

Do not apply pressure to eye or use medications without physician's advice.

- Try to remove any foreign body gently, with a moist cotton swab; if not immediately successful, get medical help. Eye pain from foreign bodies, scratches, cuts, etc., can be alleviated by patching the eye shut until a doctor's aid can be obtained.
- For chemicals splashed in eyes, flush immediately with plain water and continue washing for fifteen minutes. Do

not use drops or ointments. Call a doctor or poison control center.

- If the eye is punctured by a sharp object, do not apply pressure to lids. Consult a doctor immediately.

Nosebleeds

Have the child sit down. Squeeze outside of nostrils between thumb and index finger for ten minutes. If bleeding persists, call your physician.

Fainting

Keep patient lying down. Loosen clothing around neck. Turn head to side. Keep patient warm. Keep mouth clear. Give nothing to swallow. Obtain medical aid.

Head Injuries

Keep patient lying down. Consult a physician. Let the doctor know if:

- The child loses consciousness at any time.
- You are unable to arouse the child from sleep.
- There is persistent vomiting.
- The patient cannot move a limb.
- Blood or watery fluid oozes from the ears or nose.
- There is persistent severe headache lasting over one hour.
- There is persistent dizziness for one hour after the injury.

- The pupils of the eyes are unequally dilated.
- Patient remains abnormally pale.

Convulsions

Place child on his side in your lap. Put nothing in his mouth. Call your doctor for advice.

Index

About the Authors

Drs. Berberich and Parker have run a successful pediatric practice in Berkeley, California, for many years. Before entering private practice, Ralph Berberich was on the clinical faculty at Stanford and staff physician in pediatrics. Ann Parker serves on the teaching staff at Children's Hospital Medical Center of Northern California.